Letters from the Pandemic
Gerald O'Collins, SJ, AC

Letters from the Pandemic
Gerald O'Collins, SJ, AC

Connor Court Publishing

Letters from the Pandemic, Gerald O'Collins SJ

Published in 2022 by Connor Court Publishing Pty Ltd

Copyright © Gerald O'Collins

All rights reserved. No part of this book may be reproduced or transmitted in any form or by any means, electronic or mechanical, including photo copying, recording or by any information storage and retrieval system, without prior permission in writing from the publisher.

Connor Court Publishing Pty Ltd
PO Box 7257
Redland Bay QLD 4165
sales@connorcourt.com
www.connorcourt.com
Phone 0497-900-685

Printed in Australia

ISBN: 9781922815088

Front cover design: Maria Giordano

Praise for Letters from Rome and Beyond (Connor Court Publishing, 2021):

'One of the most prolific and representative of post-Vatican II Catholic theologians, O'Collins is also among the most affable, with a genius for friendship and networking which comes through very gently but powerfully in these pages...they are also full of interesting information, wry observation and humorous comment on theological, ecclesiastical and political matters and personalities.'
- Vivien Boland, OP, *The Pastoral Review.*

'The letters offer a window into the day-to-day life of the workings of the Catholic church from an insider living on the Tiber and an internationally recognized theologian... O'Collins is an Australian Jesuit with a personal life and with a certain freedom that comes out in these letters much more than is possible in any of his formal theological or spiritual writings. It's the nature of the writing form itself that allows for this insight that makes this collection of letters worthwhile...it's the literary form of personal letters that allows us to discover the man, his passion and his influence on theology globally that cannot be found in his formal theological books...

These letters reveal how he is equally at home writing and lecturing at the highest level of academia, supporting colleagues [on trial] at the Holy Office, writing for The Tablet and conversing with young people and family. All done in good humour and with passion for proclaiming the gospel of love and hope.'
- Revd Peter Maher, PP, *The Swag.*

'There are so many things to appreciate and value in this collection. The vivid descriptions of different cultures, the sensitivity to history near and far, the wise comments on contemporary theological concerns, the deep spirituality and love of Christ, the warmth and affection of personal relationships, and the sparks of humour throughout make for enjoyable and inspiring reading.
- Revd Canon Professor Dorothy A. Lee, *The Melbourne Anglican.*

CONTENTS

Introduction		9
1	Letters from August 2017 to January 2020	15
2	Letters from March 2020 to May 2020	35
3	Letters from June 2020 to December 2020	45
4	Letters from January 2021 to June 2021	71
5	Letters from July 2021 to December 2021	89
6	Lockdown Living	113
Some Relatives and Friends Mentioned		121
Index of Names		123

INTRODUCTION

By early 2020, COVID-19 was arriving around the world through airports, entering countries by buses, trucks, cars, and trains, or coming off ships as far away as the Argentine and New Zealand. This new economic, political, and spiritual scourge of the human race clamored for attention, and has triggered many books and articles, both popular and professional.

Community life with nine other Jesuits in Melbourne (Australia) has provided the home environment in which I experienced the pandemic playing itself out. The experience included six different lock-downs and further severe limits imposed on our normal existence and work.

We were alerted to many Jesuits, sometimes dear friends, dying from COVID-19 in Canada, India, Indonesia, Italy, the USA, and elsewhere. From June 2020 to June 2021, the virus had claimed 160 Jesuit victims. As far as I am aware, only a few Jesuits have been infected in Australia and New Zealand. But, being triple vaccinated, few felt any symptoms. Before vaccination arrived, however, the superior of my community (Steve Curtin), during a sabbatical that he spent working for refugees in Amman (Jordan) caught COVID-19, spent time in hospital, but happily recovered, returned to Melbourne in July 2021, and took up again his role of superior.

This book, through many letters I wrote (all from Jesuit Theological College, Parkville, Australia) and some I received, describes in part the coming of COVID-19 and its dispiriting impact in different corners of the world. To place the impact of the virus on 'normal' living, I include some letters, both those I sent and those I received, written *before* the corona virus arrived.

To fill out this account of life under the virus, I have included an obituary I wrote of Daniel Kendall in June 2020 and published in our co-authored book, *Jesuits, Theology, and the American Catholic Church*, an article I contributed to the Christmas 2020 issue of *The Pastoral Review*, an obituary I wrote of Hans Küng in April 2021 (also for *The Pastoral Review*), the homily which I preached at the funeral of my sister Maev in July 2021, and her obituary which I wrote for the November issue of *Theology*. All these extra items help prevent the letters that make up the heart of this book from being presented in a void.

Becoming thoroughly aware of the way COVID-19 was unsettling the world, from early 2020 I set myself to write to relatives and friends who live not only in Australia but also in other continents. I think of letters to Monica Ellison and Billy Peters in England, Jürgen Moltmann, Bernhard and Steffi Graf, and Josef and Ingrid Nolte in Germany, Nuria Calduch and Laura Zampetti in Italy, Steve Peters and his wife Marianne Lim in Malaysia, Victoria ('Tori') O'Collins in Singapore, and Brett O'Neill, Joanna Peters, and Marion Peters in the USA. In the face of the frustrations and discouragement caused by the pandemic, a cheerful letter, it seemed to me, could promise to convey some joy and hope.

Let me flag for the reader's attention some items in the different chapters and, in particular, some personal challenges to be faced as the pandemic unfolded.

Introduction

Chapter 1 opens with a letter to my beloved sister Maev, includes a round robin for Christmas 2019, but is largely made up of ten letters that formed a correspondence (from March 2019 to January 2020) between myself and a grand-niece, Genevieve ('Nevie') Peters who is studying at the University of Sydney. She has long been a dear friend, and I wanted to encourage her during the years of basic studies at Australia's oldest university (founded in 1850). The opening chapter aimed at conveying a sense of pre-pandemic, 'normal' life.

The six letters that constitute Chapter 2 all come from me, and date from March 2020 to May 2020. Addressed to different persons (in Australia and Europe), these letters reflect on COVID-19 and its impact: the aborted visits to Melbourne of my sister Maev and my lifelong friend Dan Kendall; the work of a grandnephew Billy Peters as an ambulance driver in London; the suppression of Sunday worship in Melbourne; prayers, poems and other reading for the pandemic; Pope Francis walking alone in the dark and damp of St Peter's Square; the challenge of disposing safely of COVID-19 waste for the Asian Development Bank; and doctors continuing their normal work in the face of the deadly virus.

The twelve letters that fill up Chapter 3 are overshadowed by one death (that of Dan Kendall at the very end of May) and one near death, my own. On 11 November I was admitted to Epworth Hospital (Melbourne), suffering from a thyroid gland gone amok that threatened to poison my body and overwhelm my heart. It was only thirty five days later that the hospital could discharge me. After two months of recovery spent in Campion Centre, Kew, I could return to my home at Jesuit Theological College, Parkville, on 15 February 2021.

An article on preaching Christmas under the scourge of a pandemic rounds off Chapter 3. It draws on Matthew and Luke to illustrate how Calvary had already cast its shadow over the birth of Christ in Bethlehem.

Chapter 4 reproduces letters written from January 2021 to June 2021 to friends and relatives in England, Germany. Italy, Singapore, and the USA. The chapter also includes a obituary of the Swiss theologian Hans Küng, who died on 6 April 2021.

Chapter 5, which covers July 2021 to December 2021, begins with a letter that gave me much satisfaction. A Spanish nun who taught Old Testament at the Gregorian University, Nuria Calduch Benages, had just been appointed secretary of the Pontifical Biblical Commission, the first woman to hold that prestigious position. I wrote to congratulate Nuria, not least because I opened her teaching career at the Gregorian by offering her a seminar to lead in 1991.

A sudden death on 3 July took away my beloved sister Maev, who lived the last three decades of her long life (1929–2021) in Canberra. During those years she contributed much to the Australian National University (ANU) and the local branch of the Australian Catholic University (ACU), as well as managing projects for the Australian government. The chapter includes my homily at her funeral Mass and an obituary (for the December 2021 issue of *The Expository Times*).

On 14 September 2021, we celebrated seven hundred years since Dante Alighieri died. When we test human life by what he wrote in *The Divine Comedy*, so much remains true. We continue to grieve over 'war that never sleeps' (*Purgatorio*, canto 7). Yet we also share his experience of human and divine love. Little by little, we come to share Piccarda Donati's conviction about our relationship with God: 'in his will is our peace' (*Paradiso*, canto 3).

May these letters and its final chapter (on lockdown living) share something of the spiritual journey to be revealed at the heart of every human story. I dedicate this book to the memory of my sister Maev, 'one, big, unforgettable personality' (Monica Ellison), who cheerfully poured out her life for other people right around the world.

My warm thanks to my grandniece Nevie Peters (10 letters) and those who allowed me to reproduce one letter each in this book: my cousin Monica Ellison (16 August 2021), my niece Dympna Mary Painter (18 August 2020), and a long-standing friend Laura Zampetti (24 May 2021). I have contributed 34 letters.

Gerald O'Collins, SJ, AC,

25 December 2021

Jesuit Theological College, Parkville

1
Letters from August 2017 to January 2020

Letters from August 2017 to January 2020 incorporate news and concerns before COVID-19 silently arrived. A major concern from March 2019 focused on Nevie Peters, the second daughter of my nephew Jim Peters and his wife Sally, who had just begun studies at the University of Sydney and was resident in Wesley College. There is one letter in this chapter to my sister Maev who lived in Canberra; we talked by phone once or twice a week. All the other letters, apart from a round robin at Christmas 2019, come from a correspondence between Nevie and myself.

3 August 2017.

Dearest Maev,

Last Tuesday a visiting Italian professor (now with a chair at Villanova University, near Philadelphia) came for the evening meal; he enjoys the splendid name of Massimo Faggioli, which you might translate as 'Biggest Beans'. He is an exuberant person, and has been out lecturing in Sydney, Melbourne, and Adelaide. His favorite topics are Pope Francis and the Second Vatican Council, and he has me writing a chapter for a large book he is co-editing, *The Oxford Handbook of Vatican II*.

It's certainly the season for visitors from the Northern Hemisphere, with Steve, Marianne, and Samantha through [from Singapore] for a long weekend en route to skiing in New Zealand. Last Friday Steve spoke at the students' dinner at Newman College (marking the start of the second semester) on being an engineer in Cambodia. His speech also elaborated developments aimed at setting up a national rugby team in Cambodia.

For years I have collected advertisements featuring the theme of 'life'. The latest one to be collected I spotted recently at the Melbourne airport. It featured a medical doctor saying: 'I'm not just a GP. I'm your life specialist.'

I continue to read the poems of Clive James, who has been dying on stage for several years. He's a man who has nothing but poetry left.

I have just corrected the proofs for two books, with one more set of proofs to come imminently. They will lift my list of books published to 71, which is clearly excessive, if not obsessive.

Much love, Gerald.

20 March 2019.

My dear Nevie,

I hope you have settled in very happily at your college and the university. Long live your studies in Arabic! With Sally and Jim, I have been fine tuning what we will do at the graduation of Billy [Peters, their son and Nevie's brother] and Anna [my grand-niece, Nevie's cousin, and the fourth child of Justin and Jill Peters] on Monday 29 April. I suggested to Sally that we both join the procession in our doctoral robes. [At the Australian Catholic

University (ACU) Billy graduated as a paramedic and Anna as a nurse.]

The Greek Orthodox Seminary in Sydney (Redfern) has invited me to give a lecture on Saturday 23 September. The seminary has a Catholic nun on its staff; she has been there for years, and, I think, engineered the invitation for me. On that Sydney visit, you and I may be able to get together. But I hope to see you again long before that.

On 23 May I have a book to launch here in Melbourne, on the thought of an outstanding French Dominican (Marie-Dominique Chenu). Another launch of the same book follows a week later, but in Adelaide; I can safely risk saying the same things there, since the audiences will be different.

We have three African Jesuits staying with us [at the Jesuit Theological College, Parkville] for a week or so. I hope to get one or two of them together with Sally, either with Sally coming here for lunch or my bringing one of them for a hamburger *Fest* on a Sunday evening chez Jim and Sally. [Sally had published in 2013 *Ten African Cardinals*, the result of her interviewing African church leaders in Africa and elsewhere.]

Much love, Gerald.

3 June 2019

Lieber Onkel [Dear Uncle],

I am currently sitting in college, eating an almond croissant. It's delicious but quite cold, unfortunately. I had such a lovely time at Nola's 70th last weekend; it was nice to have the family together all sitting around the table. [Nola is married to Stewart Peters, Nevie's uncle.]

I hope you've found some time to go see *All is True*, the movie about Shakespeare's life after his theatre burnt down and he retired to his family in the country. It is a great insight into 16th century England that gave me a sense of the slowness of things. Sometimes I wonder what people did with their time. Perhaps they went into town and did the shopping, took walks in the countryside, or sat and drank tea with one another. In the case of Shakespeare, he began gardening.

I have been making an effort to get outside this university suburb and explore the city. Sydney is so different to home. The biggest difference (aside from the weather) is the water. It's a bit poetic, but I would describe Sydney as an ocean city and Melbourne as a river city. [She was thinking of the river Yarra which winds its understated way through Melbourne.] In Sydney I always find myself by the bay or at the water's edge. It snakes around and I get the feeling that I am part of the rest of the world. Something about the harbor makes me feel connected internationally. Melbourne, I find, is a little more introspective. How would you say that Melbourne compares to other cities you have been to/lived in, like Rome?

My next project for the day is to find a post office and send this letter. After that I have to find a laundromat and wash my clothes. The washing machines here are not the best. Then I have to study the Cold War.

Please write back with all your news from the JTC [Jesuit Theological College]. Say hi to everyone from me.

Alles Liebe, Nevie.

9 June 2019

Liebe Nevie,

Yes, I am down to see *All is True* tomorrow at the Cinema Nova. The Bard was much loved by Patrick McMahon Glynn, your great-great-grandfather and one of Australia's founding fathers. Next Thursday the PM Glynn Institute (of the Australian Catholic University, North Sydney) launches in the Athenaeum Club (Collins Street, Melbourne) a book in collaboration about him, *Federation's Man of Letters: Patrick McMahon Glynn*. The main speaker, who has also contributed the long, biographical essay at the heart of the book, will be Anne Henderson. She is a political biographer, who has published lives of Enid Lyons, Joe Lyons, and others. You might have read her husband, Gerard Henderson; he writes every now and then for *The Australian*. Jim and Sally are coming to the launch, and I will speak, albeit briefly.

The other day I wrote to Sally Capp, the Lord Mayor of Melbourne, thanking her for what she does and making a request for Lygon Street, the Italian golden mile. Last December, instead of the banners along the street that wished you 'Buon natale', some neutral decorations (of Christmas crackers) went up. I asked the Lord Mayor to give us back at Christmas the Italian banners, which I hope have not been destroyed. Viva Italia! Viva Lygon Street. [The Italian banners never returned to Lygon Street.]

You ask about differences between Sydney and Melbourne. Did you know that in the CBD of Melbourne we have thirty bee hives and in central Melbourne 130 hives? I can't imagine that happening in Sydney, although I am not sure. I can't be sure either about the taste of the honey from Melbourne's city hives.

The Queen Victoria Market is to have a make-over costing one hundred million dollars. Well and good, but I hope this up-grading is not going to destroy the charm that draws me there on many Saturdays to buy pasta. The authorities are keeping in mind how the Queen Vic is a tourist attraction, a factor that should preserve its splendid, heritage features.

Here at the Jesuit Theological College, two seminarians—we call them scholastics—will be ordained priests next Saturday, with the ceremony taking place in St Ignatius Church, Richmond. Alas, I will be away in Canberra, celebrating Maev's 90th birthday.

Much love, Gerald.

30 August 2019

Dear Gerald,

[I am] writing to you from my desk at college. It's terribly rainy and there is some kind of pipe attached above my window, making things worse. Funnily enough, I do like the rain and the cold—it makes me feel at home. Considering that it is the last day of winter [actually second last], I don't think it will take long for the heat to set in. And besides, we need rain here at the moment.

I hope you enjoyed *All is True*. The Cinema Nova is fantastic. So is Lygon Street. I do hope they put up the Italian banners again. I reckon that would be lovely.

I think some of our letters are getting mixed up. I am responding to two letters now—one from the 30th [July?] and the other from the 6th [August]. Rest assured I have read them all. [My copies of these two letters have disappeared without a trace.] It was very cool to see the ordination invitation [an invitation to my ordination in January 1963, which turned up in my archives]. I will be keeping that one very safe.

I just finished writing a short story, Orwell-inspired, for an assignment. It was very cool to write. I am trying to move away from writing so darkly and dramatically, and I think I have had some success. I'm also trying my hand at some surrealism. There are some exceptions, like the Orwellian story I wrote. I will send it to you with this letter. It's supposed to be a kind of dystopian monologue set in 2040.

I'm also in the process of writing a creative 'Journey of the Magi' for your mate Michael McVeigh in the summer edition of *Australian Catholics*. [It appeared there and won a national, Christian award.] Maybe it will pop up in the next issue—we'll see if he likes it. Perhaps I could e-mail it to you first for some insight.

Otherwise, I enlisted on Wednesday in the army! Just the reserves. It's a small commitment with a responsibility. Wish me luck. Today I'm going to the library and will be there until my 'Great

Ideas' lecture on Simone de Beauvoir at 2 p.m. Then I think I'll post this letter.

I was also very surprised to hear about the bee hives in the city centre [of Melbourne; see letter of 9 June 2019]. Do you know that Dan Andrews [the Premier of Victoria] is thinking of closing off the CBD to all traffic? I think that would be wonderful. Maybe he could make an exception for the cheese delivery trucks at the [Queen Victoria] Market, which, by the way, I do *not* believe needs a $100,000,000 makeover. But what would I know? [Every now and then as a school girl, Nevie had worked for a cheese stall at the Market.]

Looking forward to seeing you on Thursday 19th [September], *à bientôt* [see you soon], Nevie.

PS 2 September 2019. Gerald, I have decided to send you a rough draft of the Three Kings story. I'm not sure if I should include the bit about King Herod, as I feel forced to skip over it at the end. This one is for *Australian Catholics*. Let me know your thoughts.

Nevie xx

9 September 2019.

Liebe Nevie,

Thanks for your letter and a copy of 'The Journey of the Magi', a lively retelling of the story united around Caspar. I feel like Caspar every now and then. You made me read right through the story, as did T. S. Eliot's poem 'The Journey of the Magi'. A few, minor suggestions. P. 1, three paragraphs up, two lines up: 'the men left Jerusalem [Bethlehem is in Judea, like Jerusalem.]...in pursuit of the star. That was only two days ago.' [Bethlehem is very close to Jerusalem.] Last paragraph, four lines up: panting at the doorstep. P. 2, second line 'Rising slowly to his feet'. Second last paragraph 'relayed this to his two companions. They quickly packed their bags...There was really nothing left to do.'

I look forward to reading your Orwellian monologue set in 2040. Maybe you can give me a copy on Thursday 19th? You remember how in a hospital bedroom seventy years ago he married Sonia Brownell. I began to understand what that marriage, right before Orwell died, might mean when I read an article by D. J. Taylor in the London *Tablet* for 17/24 August this year, an issue that just reached us. That was a double number, for the end of the summer holidays in the UK.

Joining the army is a great idea. Jim [Peters, her father and my nephew] explained to me what it can bring you in terms of communication skills.

I have been indulging Test cricket these days. Last night it gave me a feel-good moment when Ben Stokes walked immediately after he was caught behind by Tim Paine. Of course, he knew he was out, and any review would show that to be the case.

One of the Jesuits here in Parkville is thinking of adding some bee hives at the bottom of our back yard. As long as he knows what to do if/when a swarm takes place, all will be well and all manner of things will be well.

Much love, Gerald.

25 October 2019.

Dear Nevie,

I look forward muchly to reading your poetry, but hope you don't feel like Oscar Wilde about writing poetry. Yet I suppose he had his tongue firmly in his cheek when he expressed a wish to have a stone tablet in Oxford, 'St Oscar Wilde: Poet and Martyr'.

Nick Coleman [my nephew] has spent a week or more with Maev in Canberra; Les Coleman [his older brother] has just taken over. Annie [Coleman, my grand-niece and daughter of Dominic and Josie Coleman] may also be going up to stay. Fortunately no permanent damage has come from Maev's falls, only a tiny chip in one of her knees, which is healing, albeit slowly.

It appears that Connor Court Publishing is interested in putting out a volume of my letters: *From Rome and Beyond*. For old time's sake, I plan to end with one of my letters to you in Sydney.

I have just e-mailed the London *Tablet* a review of *The Oxford Handbook of Catholic Theology*. It shows that it was ten years in the making, as it runs to 800 pages. No, I didn't read it all, but made a sincere effort to skim at least every chapter. Most of it was well researched and written, but the indexes needed more work, Some notable authors like Bernard Lonergan featured in the book, but failed to receive a mention in the indexes. Or should it be indices?

As an alternative way of celebrating the Melbourne Cup, I plan on concelebrating at the racing Mass held in St Francis the previous Sunday. A number of owners, trainers, jockeys and concerned folk attend the Mass. Some of the owners of previous winners bring along the Melbourne Cup they received. There is a special table for those cups inside the sanctuary. The last time I attended the Melbourne Cup Mass was five years back, and I recall Michelle Payne being there in her stylish jockey's outfit and all set to win two days later.

On Cup Day itself, the plan is to turn my back on Flemington Racecourse, head for the Cinema Nova and see *Ride Like a Girl*, the film portraying Michelle Payne's triumph. A friend of mine has a non-speaking role in the film and plays the priest who says the funeral Mass for one of Michelle's sisters. That friend is a priest anyway; so he didn't have to learn how to play his part. Much love,

Gerald.

? November 2019.

Dear Gerald,

[I am] relieved to hear that Maev is okay. Or, at least, that she could be worse. I hope her knee heals soon.

I would be very interested to read some of your letters in *From Rome and Beyond*. I like to imagine you sometimes sitting on an Italian balcony, sipping espresso (or real wine) as the rising sun climbs over the peninsula. Sometimes I wish I had learned Italian; so I could sit with a little brown hat on my head and sip espresso and throw my hands around when I speak. I guess, though, that if I'd learned Italian, I might daydream about Parisian courtyards and cheeses from Provence. When I talk with my friends in France (or more likely sit in silence and try to follow the conversation), it's always a very verbal affair; we all sit still and grumble and gurgle and reflect cynically on the existentialism of life.

Really, though, I'm romanticising all of this. I've been feeling itchy to travel again and I forget the hard work that it is. A month or two in boot camp this summer should straighten me out (should everything go to plan).

What will the London *Tablet* do with your review? Publish it, I hope, so I can read it! [Nevie refers to the review of *The Oxford Handbook of Catholic Theology*, published by the *Tablet* on 9 November.] I have to remember to correctly cite all my own quotations for an upcoming essay. It's about Christopher Lasch [an American author], and there's a paragraph on religion. Maybe that can be the next thing I send you.

I hope you enjoy the Melbourne Cup Mass. Who knows—maybe you'll meet the winner again this year. I haven't been to a Catholic Mass in a little while, but I think I'll go this Sunday to a place on Broadway near Sydney University. Last week at Barney's (the Anglican Church my bible-study group goes to and benefits from), they did a kind of Anglican communion. [This is St Barnabas' Anglican Church, Broadway, near the University of Sydney.] It was great, but I miss what I'm used to. I'll get organized and head up on Sunday to St Patrick's, I think it is. It is nice getting a range, though, because as you know, it's a reminder of the same messages, just expressed in different ways.

In terms of writing, I'm taking a risk with you this week. Don't judge me too harshly please! This is a poem I wrote inspired by the Grand Final [in Australian Football League] and (some of) the guys who watch it. I don't really know what I'm doing. Write back soon,

Nevie.

PS Is 'unawakened' a word?

> 'Saturdays in Moorabbin [a suburb of Melbourne]'.
> Would you look at them, slumped/unawakened by the rising sun.
> Its shadow climbs over their drooling heads,/The gilded youth, the irony.
> See how sitting there, leaning/forward, shouting, waving
> One mighty, hard worn finger/you crab! You filthy yellow maggot!
> As if his lengthy screams might make it/Through the wind and move the ball itself.
> He picks up the footy and sprints./Push it, Digger. Digger, run!
> Tumbles, slams it down, kicks it./He is black with dirt;/the crowd erupts.
> A crusty, yellow eye/ squints into the light that he does not like.
> The rising sun a reminder of his dreaded failure.
> He wants to believe he should roam in the night,/That realm of shift workers, possums and criminals, /That realm to which he does not belong.
> It hurts him to be struck by reality./That's not his territory, it's theirs./It hurts.

7 November 2019

Dear Nevie,

Yes, 'unawakened' is a word to be used; it even enjoys, at least for me, a Shakespearean echo. Now I need to re-read your poem several times more. Instant evaluations of a poem, like instant judgments of a painting are to be avoided. As an e-mail attachment, I will send you some of those letters from Rome.

A cardinal in Rome, who is charged with interreligious relations, has asked me to contribute a chapter to a book he is editing on Buddhist-Christian dialogue. My knowledge of Buddhism is dreadfully superficial, nothing like the deep appreciation of Buddhism revealed by some Jesuits in Sri Lanka and Japan. I think I have found a way of saying something moderately useful without betraying my deplorable ignorance.

Last Sunday the racing fraternity, led by Amanda Elliott, the long-time president (or is she secretary?) of the Victorian Racing Club, attended the 9.30 Mass at St Francis' Church. She read the first lesson. (During a slice of my life, I used to go every four years to her brother-in-law's clinic in East Melbourne for a colonoscopy. He found nothing and so I am still here.) Up to the offertory procession, the 2019 Melbourne Cup stood alone on a table in the sanctuary; then, along with the gifts of bread and wine, previous Melbourne Cups were brought up by their owners/winners and covered the table. Incidentally the trainer of the 2019 winner is an old-Xaverian. His horse was one of the two Australian horses in the race. [Xavier College is the high school attended by Nevie's father, myself, and many of my family.] The rest came from Ireland, Japan, New Zealand etc. After Mass on Sunday, I had a yarn with the New Zealand couple who own The Chosen One, and expressed my hope that their horse might win the race. But TCO ran nowhere.

Sip some coffee when you sample my letters, and see whether/how Lavazza improves their flavour. It's now 7.45 a.m., and I must return to Buddhism.

Much love, Gerald.

December 2019

[This Christmas letter was sent to many relatives and friends.]

With tongue firmly in his cheek, the Irish genius James Joyce said of John Henry Newman: 'nobody has ever written English prose that can be compared with that of a tiresome footling little Anglican parson who afterwards became a prince of the only true Church.' It was a great joy to be alive for Newman's canonization on 13 October 2019. I hope and pray for a blazing exception to normal practice, and see Newman's writings prompt his entering the most select group of saints by being officially proclaimed the thirty-seventh Doctor of the Church.

My beloved sister Maev, the only other survivor of my parents' six children, was awarded earlier this year by the Australian Catholic University an honorary doctorate. I could not share that occasion on 12 April. But I happily visited Canberra to celebrate her ninetieth birthday on 16 June, the famous Bloom's Day of Joyce's *Ulysses*.

As one of their chaplains, the Order of Malta keeps me pastorally engaged with visits to retirement homes around Melbourne and a respite centre for old Italians in Kew. At the end of November, along with Archbishop Jean Laffitte (their official prelate), several of the supreme council of the Order visited from Rome for an Asia Pacific Conference. Laffitte, when a student at the French Seminary, had been my student at the Gregorian University. After not seeing each other for 35 years, he hugged me and greeted me warmly as 'professore'.

As the world knows, the annual Melbourne Cup is THE racing event in Australia. This year I attended the Mass—in fact concelebrated—for the racing fellowship in St Francis' Church, Melbourne's oldest, CBD church on 4 November, two days before the Cup (always held on the first Tuesday of November). Numerous owners, trainers, jockeys, and other concerned folk attended the Mass. Some owners brought along the cups they had won in previous years; inside the sanctuary there was a special table for all those cups. The last time I attended the Cup Mass, Michelle Payne (see the film *Ride Like a Girl*) attended in her stylish jockey's outfit and was all set to win the Cup on an outsider (one hundred to one) two days later.

In mid-2020 Oxford University Press will publish my *The Beauty of Jesus Christ*. Around the same time, Paulist Press (Mahwah, New Jersey) will put out a book I have co-authored with Daniel Kendall: *Jesuits, Theology, and the American Catholic Church*.

Interest in my maternal grandfather is being promoted by the PM Glynn Institute of Australian Catholic University. This year the institute published Anne Henderson's *Federation's Man of Letters* (Kapunda Press; Connor Court Publishing), which argued that Paddy Glynn's life, inspiration, intellectual heroes, and ideas remain powerfully relevant in debates that continue about Australia's identity and future. One of the founding fathers of Australian federation, until 1919 he remained in the national parliament and was a cabinet minister in several governments. In September, on the occasion of a visit to Australia, Archbishop Rowan Williams delivered in Sydney the annual PM Glynn lecture.

A blessed Christmas and every grace in the New Year, Gerald

Late January 2020

[*This letter was written shortly before Billy Peters, my grand-nephew, and his partner Emma left for London where he began working as a paramedic and driving an ambulance—just in time for the outbreak of the pandemic. Neddy Coleman, another grand-nephew, left for work/study in Indonesia.*]

Liebe Nevie,

It was very good to catch up once again on the eve of the exodus of Billy, Emma, and Neddy. I hope the Oz army [reserve] has received you with open arms and not too much boot camp hardship.

These last few days, I have been struggling with the process of submitting an article to *The Scottish Journal of Theology*. It used to be simple: an e-mail to the editor, with the article attached, sufficed. But now you have to transmit a university ID and all kinds of details that the Open Athens system requires. It seems more like a Closed Athens system, in which you contend with an anonymous system rather than enter into dialogue with an editor. What would Socrates and Plato say, not to mention Aristotle?

Maev was on the phone the other day, and reported no damage after the fierce hail storm which hit Canberra.

I used to think that the BBC gave the best tennis coverage of a slam, when Sue Barker, John McEnroe, Pat Cash etc presented the Wimbledon championships. But I am weakening towards assigning in my mind the # 1 position to Channel Nine, with friendly Jim Courier and the others sharing all the fun and battles taking place at Melbourne Park [for the Australian Open].

My mottos are currently two, one secular and the other sacred. First, meet face to face, see eye to eye, and smile ear to ear. Then, borrowed from St Paul, 'for me to live is Christ' (Philippians 1:21).

Over at Newman College [across the campus of Melbourne University from where I live at Jesuit Theological College], the arrival of the new rector, has brought—or at least been accompanied by—a new carpet in the chapel and, more importantly, a shift of the Sunday choral Mass from 7 in the evening to 11 a.m. They have a good choir, not as good as that of St Francis's Church [a church in the CBD of Melbourne] but still good enough to go on tour in Europe. Cry your heart out, St Francis's; I will be going to Newman more often. [In the event, the lockdowns prompted by COVID-19 frequently ruled out attending the Sunday morning Eucharist at Newman College.]

All the army best to you and *viele Gruesse* (many greetings),

Gerald.

31 January 2020.

Lieber Gerald,

Thank you for writing! It [your letter] found me, For future reference, I am 42 Platoon, Echo Company. This letter may take a moment to find you. I left my stamped envelopes in my 'civvie' bag' which is locked away downstairs. I'll have to find the right moment to approach my scary corporals about the issue.

Isn't bureaucracy such a drag? Because of an admin issue, the University of Sydney claims I did not enroll in a French subject (which I undertook all semester) and won't give me my mark or the records on my transcript. That's an issue for future me, though I understand your pain regarding your article.

Boot camp has been interesting so far. There is much talk of 'standards' and 'discipline', which I understand now that we are handling weapons. You can't give a bunch of excited 18-year-olds assault rifles and expect everything to be fine and dandy.

There is limited free time. In fact, this is the first opportunity I've had to write any letters. We have some interesting characters here at Kapooka. Our corporals, for example, each with a different story, all of them younger than forty, but with a very dry sense of humor that reminds me of Dom [Coleman, a nephew of mine who died in mid-2019]. We have our platoon sergeant as well, who to me has two faces: one, a scary, screaming shadow with a feather in his cap, pacing furiously up and down the lines at eleven p.m., while we all look on, petrified, from our attention positions on the side of the hallway. The other is a friendly man, hat off, delivering us lessons, again with that dry sense of humor. Each recruit has their own personality as well, and most are kind and encouraging and optimistic, which is nice. The other night at dinner I had to rush out of the mess hall and this young guy I had never spoken to, without a word, upon my nervous confusion, simply picked up my cutlery and crockery and walked away with it. Also, two female recruits just gave me a stack of pre-stamped letters to use. Funny how kindness can flourish in the harshest situations!

With that, I'll leave you to it: keep writing if you come across any interesting article or anything [else]. We are very removed from the world here; so any news is appreciated.

Mit ganz vieler Liebe [with very much love], *deine* Nevie [your Nevie].

2

Letters from March 2020 to May 2020

These six letters, all written by me, show COVID-19 beginning to condition life at every level and around the world, especially in Asia, Australia, Europe, and the USA.

6 March 2020.

Dear Nevie,

Last night Sally and Jim took me to the Cinema Nova to see *Emma*, a costume drama in which the father of Emma (Bill Nighy) and the wife of the vicar (I can't recall the name of the actress) ran away with the story. Sally brought along your letter to me [of 31 January 2020], which filled me in about life in Echo Company, 42 Platoon. I was delighted to hear about corporals, the platoon sergeant, and amiable recruits, but sorry that the University of Sydney declines to release your French results. I hope that by this time they have repented of their wicked ways. The photos of you are wonderful and reveal a born soldier.

A Jesuit friend of mine [Daniel Kendall] from the University of San Francisco has been edging his way towards arriving in Melbourne on the morning of 2 April. So far, having left Rome for Mombai (where he is staying with two Indians who studied with him at the Biblical Institute in Rome), he is just ahead of one Australian ban, the ban on passengers from Italy. But we still have a month to go, and I don't want him arriving at Tullamarine airport [Melbourne] and being compelled to face two weeks of quarantine, even self-imposed and self-administered quarantine. An even worse scene would be his being forbidden to board the flight from Singapore to Melbourne on the evening of 1 April.

[Dan skipped Australia, returned to San Francisco, faced a quarantine period there, and emerged seemingly quite healthy. But then he suddenly collapsed, and died in a Jesuit infirmary in Los Gatos, California, on 26 May.]

Last Sunday's evening meal was blessed by the presence of three people with Down's Syndrome, plus two doctors (husband and wife, and both still intensely Welsh after many years in Hobart and Melbourne) and the L'Arche assistant who runs the home where the folk with Down's Syndrome live. L'Arche is a worldwide organization with around eight houses in Australia; it provides a residence for those with intellectual disabilities, who often suffer also from physical disabilities.

Maev will visit Melbourne later this month, and I am rounding up relatives to lunch with her at the Clyde Hotel (Carlton) on Saturday 21 March. [Because of COVID-19, she never came.] Nick Coleman is a shining agent in bringing her down from Canberra, but does not always inform everyone about the details of her visits. Maybe it's the philosopher in him.

Much love, Gerald.

March 15, 2020.

[A letter sent to the London Tablet but not published.]

After graduating as a paramedic in 2019 at the Australian Catholic University (Melbourne), William ('Billy') Peters, a grand-nephew of mine, accepted a job with the London paramedics. He began work at the end of January, just in time for the arrival of the corona virus. These uniquely busy and tragic months have pushed Billy to the limit of his resources. But he has been mightily encouraged by the British public repeatedly demonstrating their gratitude to all health-care workers. Last week this support was dramatically confirmed for him in a very personal way. He lost his wallet in a London pub.

The lady who picked it up found inside his American Express Card and utterly essential driver's licence, but no contact details for Billy. The wallet contained, however, the card of his father, a Melbourne barrister James Peters, QC. Her e-mail to Billy's dad produced instant results. Billy went at once, with enormous relief and gratitude, to retrieve his precious wallet from a London stranger. He is now more dedicated than ever to his work in London as a paramedic. PS Yes, Billy has been infected by the virus, but, being in his early twenties, shook it off easily.

March 29, 2020.

[To my nephew Frank O'Collins, Sydney.]

Dear Frank,

We don't have a lockdown [yet] in Melbourne, but often people are short on the streets, with only a few scuttling about. Right here on Royal Parade in Parkville, the shutting of a redbrick church for members of a community of St Thomas Christians has made our Sunday mornings much quieter and less colourful. A few years ago they bought a church that had been built around 1900 on the model of an old church in Scotland and served as a place of worship for local Presbyterians, members of Ormond College (just across Royal Parade), and latterly a few members of the Uniting Church of Australia. At the Jesuit community, 157—175 Royal Parade, we found our Sunday brightened by cars arriving from around Melbourne, flocks of Indian ladies in saris (with the men often dressed much more casually), and bunches of small children. They began at 9 am or earlier and continued all Sunday morning, using the church itself and the adjacent lawn. Twenty or so teenagers would come to one of our terrace buildings, 175 Royal Parade, and occupy a classroom for their lessons in catechism. Recently the Indians invited our superior [Steve Curtin] to preach at a Sunday morning liturgy. All in all, those St Thomas Christians made our Sundays lively, festive occasions. Now Sunday morning seems thoroughly sombre.

I have been collecting poems and prayers that the corona virus has prompted. You must have read 'Lockdown' by Richard Hendrick, OFM, which turned up on the BBC recently and has followed the virus around the world: 'Yes, there is fear. Yes, there is isolation. Yes, there is panic buying. Yes, there is sickness. Yes, there is even death. But they say that in Wuhan after so many years of noise/You can hear the birds again. They say that after a few weeks of quiet/ The sky is no longer thick with fumes/But blue and grey and clear. They say that in the streets of Assisi/People are singing to each other/across the empty squares...'

The latest prayers often don't quite live up to that standard. In the present, viral situation, I still like best a prayer from St Anselm of Canterbury (d. 1109): 'God of love, whose compassion never fails, we bring before you the troubles and perils of people and nations, the sighing of prisoners and captives, the sorrows of the bereaved, the necessities of strangers, the helplessness of the weak, the despondency of the weary, the failing powers of the aged. O Lord, draw near to each; for the sake of Jesus Christ our Lord.'

Some of my friends have turned back to reading again Albert Camus's *The Plague*. What I recall most and recall sadly about the novel is that, after all the fears and deaths abate, the survivors hardly seem to have been changed by their experiences of a city in lockdown for months.

Peace and love, Gerald.

30 March 2020.

[*To the Princess Gesine and Massimiliano Doria Pamphilj, Rome.*]

Dear Gesine, Massimiliano, and all your dear ones,

Hearing the news from Italy and the terrible toll the corona virus has already taken, I have been thinking of you and praying for you.

Here in Melbourne we are blessed with three interesting heavenly patrons or at least temporary patrons: St Thérèse of Lisieux and her two (canonized) parents. Some time back their relics left France on a world tour, and reached Melbourne just as the corona virus began causing lockdowns. Now the relics remain for an undetermined time in the local Carmelite monastery. May the saintly Martin family roll back the virus and its impact from this city!

You must have seen Pope Francis in St Peter's Square last Friday. It looked so strange, even surreal, to watch him walking alone through the wet and deserted square—a tiny, white figure in the darkness. He excelled himself with the homily and its message, 'with God life never dies'.

I hope and pray, Gesine, that the cancer has diminished or even disappeared. You might remember in your prayers my sister Maev, now ninety and living hundreds of miles away in Canberra. She has generous and loving neighbours, but I wish she was down here in Melbourne where most of her close relatives live. I spend my time doing some translation work—specifically, putting into English some passages from documents from the Second Vatican Council—and writing articles. It's all a good distraction from the general nervousness that the corona virus has caused,

Much love to each of you, Gerald.

21 April 2020.

[To Josef and Ingrid Nolte, Tübingen, Germany.]

Dear Josef, Ingrid, and all your dear ones,

I hope everything is going well, despite the corona virus. I think we're stuck with this virus for a long haul, but it only makes friends like you even more precious. In January a grandnephew, Billy Peters, arrived in London to begin work as paramedic; he graduated a year ago from the Australian Catholic University and the authorities in the UK are happy with the courses at ACU. He is coping with an extraordinary start to his career—much encouraged by the ways the British public is expressing thanks to health care workers. A nephew (Steve), an engineer in his early fifties who has worked for years on waste management in South-East Asia and lives (with wife and daughter) in Malaysia, is flat out designing ways of disposing safely (and maybe profitably) of COVID-19 waste for the Asian Development Bank.

While Billy and Steve are at the front, I am locked away in the Jesuit Theological College with seven others, including one who graduated in medicine before becoming a Jesuit. It is reassuring to live next door to a doctor at this viral time. Two of the other Jesuits were lawyers before they entered the Society, and have been keeping the rest of us accurate and informed in what we discuss about the Cardinal George Pell case. He was hardly acquitted 7/0 by the Australian High Court, before someone else apparently (police leak!) contacted the police about another offence allegedly committed in the 1970s.

No doubt about our coppers; they will not quit on getting their man.[1] A youngish American friend, a lay theologian, sent me, for Easter, links to recordings of nine heavy metal, Christian bands. A kind gesture, but I cannot remember ever showing interest in heavy metal bands, Christian or otherwise.

I potter away writing articles of a biblical nature for the *Expository Times* and other journals. It's a case of '*il primo amore non si scorda mai* (one's first love never becomes unravelled)'. I prefer the Italian to the English version of this saying; it brings out love's activity, rather than its memory ('you never forget your first love'). Scriptures were my first love, and so I've come back to them. Oxford University Press publish this month my *The Beauty of Jesus Christ*.

With warmest Easter greetings, affection, and prayer, Gerald.

17 May 2020.

[To Mary Venturini, living no longer in Rome but on the island of Jersey.]

Dear Mary,

A very grace-filled feast of the Ascension next Thursday. Years ago you wrote such a wonderful section on the Ascension for *Believing* [a book we published together in 1991]; I sensed that it was a special liturgical feast for you. You must know the Beaulieu Convent School [on Jersey]? I think an old friend of mine, Paul Rowan, is

---

1 See Frank Brennan, *Observations on the Pell Proceedings* (Brisbane: Connor Court Publishing, 2021). In a case that many thought should never have come to court, since the evidence for Cardinal Pell having committed child sexual abuse was impossibly weak, the failures of the Victorian police, prosecution authorities, and Victoria's two most senior judges were blatant.

still teaching there. We met in Rome and then caught up at St Mary's University College, Strawberry Hill, Twickenham.

Despite the pandemic, Dr Willie Campbell (yes, he was born in Scotland where he also did his basic training in medicine), who lasered my left eye three months ago, has not shut up shop. Last week he lasered my right eye, and now both eyes enable me to read happily and without glasses. Am I grateful for the progress of medicine and the skill of Willie, who served as a resident under my late brother Jim (the head surgeon of a Melbourne hospital) after migrating years ago to Australia!

At this Jesuit precinct opposite the University of Melbourne, we continue to see the best of films and engage in thoughtful discussions that may train us to be top (or maybe only mediocre) cinema critics. On Friday evening it was *The King*, a kind of alternative to Shakespeare's *Henry V*. Impossible to see without thinking of the classical performances of Kenneth Branagh and Laurence Olivier as Henry V, the film did its job under an Australian director and was shot in Hungary.

During the reign of the virus, I am able to catch up with a favourite BBC Sunday program, 'Songs of Praise'. Last Sunday a Coptic church in London was on; the Sunday before the program took us to Tenby beach and the very old (fifth century) monastery on Caldey Island, off the coast of Wales.

Peace, love and Ascension blessings to you, Gerry.

3

Letters June 2020 to December 2020

2 June 2020.

[*To Paulist Press, just in time for insertion into Daniel Kendall and Gerald O'Collins, Jesuits, Theology and the American Catholic Church.*]

Born Miami, Arizona, 11 January 1939, Daniel Kendall died Los Gatos, California, 26 May 2020. I first met Dan in Rome when he was a recently ordained Jesuit priest, living at the Collegio Bellarmino and studying for his licentiate in Sacred Scripture at the Pontifical Biblical Institute. He relished life in Rome, and delighted in the teaching of Carlo Maria (later Cardinal) Martini and other professors. With his licentiate at the Biblicum finished, he then crossed the street to the Pontifical Gregorian University. He successfully completed a doctorate with me (on several Church Fathers applying to purgatory what Paul said in 1 Corinthians 3:13–15), the first of nearly one hundred students to write and defend a doctoral dissertation with me—my *primogenito* (first born), as Dan liked to describe himself.

I began full time teaching at the Gregorian in 1974, and Dan returned to the United States. He taught at the University of San Francisco from 1979 and for at least six years chaired its Department of Theology and Religious Studies. We never lost touch, and Dan often hosted me as a visiting professor at the USF summer program. He joined me in writing articles that appeared in *Biblica* (1994), *Catholic Biblical Quarterly* (1992), *Gregorianum* (1993, 1994), *Heythrop Journal* (1996), *Scottish Journal of Theology* (1994), and *Theological Studies* (1987, 1992). Dan built on that experience when he served as book review editor for *Theological Studies* (2012-19).

We started writing and editing books together: *The Bible for Theology* (Paulist Press, 1997); *In Many and Diverse Ways*, a Festschrift in honor of Jacques Dupuis on his 80th birthday (Orbis, 2003); and four volumes edited with Stephen Davis, published by Oxford University Press and coming from interdisciplinary conferences held in New York, *The Resurrection* (1997), *The Trinity* (1999), *The Incarnation* (2002), and *The Redemption* (2004). With Steve Davis, Dan edited a Festschrift for my 70th birthday, *The Convergence of Theology* (Paulist Press, 2001). Jeffrey LaBelle joined Dan and myself in preparing *Pope John Paul II: A Reader* (Paulist Press, 2007). Then the three of us edited *Seek God Everywhere* (Doubleday, 2010), lectures on the *Spiritual Exercises* delivered by Anthony de Mello. Now the last book that Dan and I co-authored or co-edited, *Jesuits, Theology and the American Catholic Church*, is about to appear with Paulist Press. In my own name and that of Dan I want to warmly thank the Paulist Press and its Senior Academic Editor, Donna Crilly.

Dan was the epitome of friendship, encouragement, and fun. Nothing delighted him more than sitting down for a meal with those he loved. I am so glad that in 2019 he was enabled to spend the major part of a sabbatical back at the Collegio Bellarmino, visit his favorite places in Rome, and meet (and be photographed with) Pope Francis. Dan never failed to plan carefully his flights, so that he could catch up with old friends in India, the Philippines, Australia, and elsewhere. Sadly, at the start of March this year the spread of the corona virus forced him to fly straight home to San

Francisco from Manila (via Singapore) rather than make a detour and stay with me in Melbourne.

For nearly fifty years I was nourished by the friendship of Dan, and shared him with relatives and others. He was one of the very best friends and academic colleagues I have ever enjoyed. To his sister Anne, his deceased parents, and the Society of Jesus in the United States, I wish to express my sincere thanks for bringing Dan into my life and through him blessing me in so many ways. While I pray for Dan, I am sure he is already delighting in the wonderful, total friendship that is heavenly life, a friendship that will never, never end. RIP.

Those who came to know Dan quickly became conscious of his uncomplicated, deep love for the Society of Jesus and for Jesuits, both at home in the United States and around the world. God's providence has seen to it that his last and posthumous book describes and warmly evaluates what Jesuits have done in North America to develop and share life-giving and truth-enhancing theology in its various branches.

14 June 2020.

[To Monsignor Bernard McGarty, La Crosse, Wisconsin.]

Dear Bernie,

Many thanks for your card, which gives me this chance of contacting you. First of all, my deep condolences and prayers on the death of your dear and wonderful sister. R.I.P. I remain immensely grateful to you for bringing me to Wisconsin. Those visits from the early nineties up to 2006 were full of grace and joy for me.

These days of lock-down in the face of the pandemic are not what I expected from 2020. But there have been the lovely items, like a priest from Shanghai who joined my birthday celebration and sang in mandarin 'happy birthday to you'. The tune, by the way, is the same. The government, if slowly, is lifting restrictions. The Melbourne Zoo, just north of where I live, is re-opened; the animals must have missed us and demanded our return. But, since the number of visitors is limited and you go on line to book a ticket, signs en route to the zoo warn those who have not yet booked with the message 'ZOO FULL'

Oxford University Press has just published my *The Beauty of Jesus Christ*. So I have started on another book—eighteen articles on New Testament topics which I authored or co-authored over the years. For the first five years after completing my PhD, I taught the letters of St Paul, along with a course in fundamental theology, for Weston School of Theology (then Cambridge, Massachusetts). But departmental arrangements meant that I had to stay with the theologians (fundamental and systematic) when I moved to Rome; nevertheless, every now and then I published a scriptural article in *Biblica*, *Catholic Biblical Quarterly*, *Expository Times* or some other journal. So I am revising the earlier pieces and bringing them up to date. More than half appeared in recent years and hardly call for any retouching. Provisionally, I am calling this collection: *Expounding the New Testament: The Gospels, Acts and Paul*. As Oxford University Press declined to take the book, I am negotiating with another publishing house.

Thanks again for everything, and all the very, very best in the good Lord, Gerald. PS Paulist Press will shortly publish a book I co-authored with Daniel Kendall: *Jesuits, Theology and the American Catholic Church*. You will know some of those scholars and priests recalled in it.

28 July 2020

[To Lady Primrose Potter, Melbourne.]

Dear Primrose,

Well, here we are five months down the pandemic track in defending ourselves against the 'opportunistic psychopath' as one journalist has described the corona virus. Dan Andrews [the premier of the State of Victoria] went for alliteration when he denounced Covid-19 as a 'very complex, cunning, and clever enemy'. But should one personify a virus? Whatever we say, I hope you are well and truly guarded against the enemy.

Advice, prayers and quotations have arrived in a steady stream through my computer. A quote received recently comes from A. A. Milne, *Winnie the Pooh*: 'promise me you will always remember you're braver than you believe, and stronger than you seem, and smarter than you think'. Covid-time has proved cliché-time. Yet some sentiments appeal: 'the role of economic forecasting is to make astrology seem respectable'.

The pandemic makes some ads unconsciously amusing, like one (in *The Economist*) for a property in Tuscany: 'don't just own it. Live it. Now is your chance to create a life in the real Tuscany, in a land untouched by time'. In September 2021 we will celebrate 700 years since the death of Dante. I wonder what he would think about Tuscany being a land untouched by time. It's precisely because it is a land touched by time that it's so interesting and beautiful.

Furthermore, what on earth is the unreal Tuscany, as opposed to the real Tuscany?

Yesterday in an e-mail my nephew Jim Peters quoted to me

something very apposite from Catullus. I started noting his preference for the Latin lyric poets when he first visited me in Rome and wanted to see the places that inspired Horace. I am firmly in the epic camp of Virgil: *'sunt lacrimae rerum et mentem mortalia tangunt'*. It sounds banal in English: 'there are tears for things' ('human affairs?', 'the human story?') 'and mortal things touch the mind' ('heart' might be better).

Covid-time is making me more alert to quirky bits of information like that about a Brisbane church built of concrete in the 1960s, which has just won 'the Enduring Architecture Award' in the annual assignment of Queensland architecture awards. That seems a tautology, or is an oxymoron involved? Since the building is made of concrete, it should be sturdily there fifty or sixty years down the track.

Peace, love, and good cheer, Gerald.

July 2020

[This fragment comes from a letter written in July 2020 and obviously addressed to a reader of the London Tablet.]

...Well, as you can see from the latest *Tablet*, Brendan Walsh [editor] published my letter on the von Teuffenbach/Tromp connection. Yesterday the post managed to deliver four weeks' issues—a record. But for the 18 July number, I relied on digital arrangements, and could confirm that, despite Brendan's enigmatic response to me some days back, *there* was the letter.²

Last Tuesday I watched for a second time *A Sense of an Ending*, and once again applauded the acting of Jim Broadbent, Charlotte Rampling, Michelle Dockery (Lady Mary in *Downton Abbey*), and the rest. But seeing it now in a year when that opportunistic psychopath—to steal a phrase from a local journalist—the corona virus has its grip on our throat (read lungs) gave the film a fresh urgency. I felt Julian Barnes's novel and the film offer an example of what Philip Larkin (a friend or at least an acquaintance of his) might have meant by 'what will remain of us is love'). Love came through the birth of a child to Tony's daughter, at which he assisted, and the care that a very decent young man showed to half a dozen intellectually disabled persons. In a kind way he let Tony know that the Adrian in his charge was not the brother of Veronica (Tony's early girl friend) but her half brother. Without going into details, I felt Barnes had done a George Eliot (was it in *Vanity Fair*?) and transferred a relationship from a daughter to a mother. The whole story remains so low key, offering merely 'a' sense of an ending, and leaving so many dots to be connected. It rather suits modern times and this latest dramatic episode, a bleak, pandemic present. But somehow love has redeemed crusty, old Tony, 'Mudge'

---

2   Entitled 'Same Doubtful Team?', this letter stated:
    'Alexandra von Teuffenbach is an admirable person, and so too was the late Fr Sebastiaan Tromp on whose reports she relies for accusations of abusive behaviour made against the founder of the Schoenstatt Community, Fr Josef Kentenich (*Tablet*, 2 July). She also relied on Tromp to interpret Vatican II as teaching that the Church founded by Christ 'exists only (*subsistit*)' in the Catholic Church (Dogmatic Constitution on the Church, 8). She enlisted the diary kept by Tromp during the Council to support finding that meaning in 'subsistit'. Many commentators, however, understand Vatican II to have taught that the Church founded by Christ 'exists fully' or 'exists concretely' in the Catholic Church—a 'lesser' and more accurate claim than 'exists only'. Memories of that earlier debate about '*subsistit*' could make one cautious about accepting the latest news from the von Teuffenbach/Tromp team. Gerald O'Collins, SJ, Jesuit Theological College, Parkville, Australia'.

(short for Curmudgeon) to his daughter...

5 August 2020.

[To Nevie Peters]

Dear Nevie,

Welcome out of the quarantine and back to the University of Sydney campus. Down here in Victoria, the premier and others indulge their fashion of personifying the virus: 'it is a very silent enemy and a very cunning enemy'. The local news assured us that the 'virus exploits any weakness we've got'. I hope you may have finished Marcel Proust [*In Search of Lost Time*] before emerging from quarantine.

Viele Gruesse, Gerald.

6 August 2020.

Lieber Gerald,

thanks for your distanced welcome. I got back to college yesterday afternoon, and have been getting used to the swing of things here. It is very different with only an eighth or so of the normal population. There are only a few people at meals at a time. The college is quiet (no parties all hours of day or night) and people seem extra friendly. Those I had never spoken to all of last year I now sit next to at lunch, and we talk like we have known each other for ages. It's very interesting. I hope it stays this way, but sadly everybody will be coming back in a few weeks, and that might break the magic.

I have Arabic tutoring today. My lovely Syrian tutor spends an hour with me every week reading children's stories and teaching me vocabulary. It has been a delayed lesson this week; so I am looking forward to getting back to it.

I really feel for you all down South. At least it's an interesting case study as to how politicians handle crises. I suppose you have lived through the Vietnam War, the Cuban Missile Crisis, the Korean War, aboriginal and women's liberation movements, and more, and so you have lots to compare. This is just the start for me really.

You sent that lovely poem to me in a letter which I found in the 'P' pigeon hole last night [presumably the poem found above in a letter for 29 March 2020]. A good reminder to stay positive, calm and, above all, kind. I think that's what people and college are doing now, talking to each other and treating one another like friends as opposed to stepping stones in the social hierarchy (although, I hate to say it, some remain [like that]).

The terrible news from Lebanon [the Beirut port explosion of 4 August 2020] has left me feeling a bit rattled. People from my Arabic class have family and friends who have passed away. Our group chat is full of Arabic expressions of grief and support, passages about love from the *Quran*, and lots of empathy for those of us going through a hard time. Hopefully Lebanon will be able to find its feet again.

[I am] looking at the oval through my college window now, and the eternal Sydney sun that shines through all the leaves and Moreton Bay fig trees. As the poem goes, 'yes, there is death, but there can always be a rebirth of love'.

Liebe Gruesse, Nevie.

17 August 2020.

[To the theologian Jürgen Moltmann, Tübingen, Germany.]

Dear Jürgen,

I hope all has gone well for you, and all your dear ones. As you will have seen in the news, Melbourne is back to a more severe lockdown, involving a curfew (8 pm to 5 am), wearing masks, and soldiers on the streets to enforce these and other regulations. Through the window of my second-floor study, I have just seen an army patrol pass by.

Last week I was one of the ten persons allowed to attend the requiem Mass of a New Zealand friend, celebrated in a large suburban church. Everyone was masked, including Michael Tobin, the well preserved, silky white-haired, now semi-retired director of an agency. For many years he has presided over the funerals of numerous relatives and friends of mine. Always in a perfect suit, with a matching tie and handkerchief, Michael fits his role perfectly. But last week even he could not manage to look the part. The mask distracted you totally from his formal 'uniform'.

With all outside activities, including visits to relatives and friends, forbidden, I have been driven to do more reading and writing. Fortunately, some invitations from editors have come along to satisfy the urge to write. The latest request [from Australian Theological Forum] asked for 6,000 words on what my theology has achieved. Answering such a request looks daunting in the extreme. But at least I can confirm that teaching and writing theology have kept me contented. Declaring what that activity has done for others lurches into the controversial.

A desire to read has taken me back to Homer and Vergil. I started with the *Iliad* but then switched to the *Aeneid*. You remember its opening words, '*arma virumque cano* (I sing of arms and the man'), which years ago were adopted as the motto of the classics department at the University of Melbourne and appeared on their stationery? Some truly ignorant individual in search of a teaching position took the words to be the full name of the professor who headed the department and opened his letter by writing: 'Dear Professor Cano'. Needless to say, he was not taken on.

An abundance of time has also prompted me into reading novels that I have kept in my room but never opened. As of now I have finished the first of a quartet by Martin Boyd, an Australian writer who eventually lived near the Trevi Fountain and died in Rome in 1979. Daffodils, mimosa, and other flowers, as well as sunny days, are signalling that spring is on the way. The sooner the summer arrives to check the corona virus, the better.

In alter Freundschaft, Gerry.

18 August 2020.

[*A letter from a widowed niece, Dympna Mary Painter, to another niece, Bronwen Peters, on the occasion of Bronwen's birthday. The eight Peters siblings, plus some other relatives, have the admirable habit of circulating such letters to a fuller list of relatives. In this case, I received a copy, along with fourteen others.*]

Dear Brony,

I feel lucky to be here on the Bass Coast [South-East of Melbourne], lots of space, clean air and wonderful creatures, apart from Terri the terrible tiger snake who took residence under a flower pot outside my back door. A kind neighbour has since relocated him. I felt sad to know I would never see his cute, little, snake eyes peering out at me anymore. Carly [her daughter] said that I was obviously suffering from Stockholm Syndrome.

I have totally embraced lockdown; only stage three at the Gurdies; so no army here—yet. A delightful gentleman delivers my groceries at the press of a few buttons. Click and collect at the big green shed means I don't even have to get out of the car. I have enough clay [for pottery] to see me through until next year and plenty to do in the garden. So I'm thinking I never have to leave home again in 2020.

[I] am taking delivery of a Wollemi pine tomorrow, a bit exciting; [I] hope it looks as healthy as those Illawarra flame trees.

Cheers to all and a very happy birthday, Brony, DM *[Dympna Mary]*.

30 August 2020.

Liebe Nevie,

With your birthday coming up on 4 September, let me offer you proleptically (what a word!) every best wish. I have been pondering the significance of your age of twenty in the year 2020. 20/20 should mean something deeply special. But, apart from a link to cricket, I remain unsure what the meaning might be.

Prompted by a friend, a former speech writer for Malcolm Fraser, I have been trying to come up with a popular song to lift the spirits of people who are suffering from lockdown blues. So far only a few words have popped into my head to match a tune taken from 'Men of Harlech': 'Team Australia, do your share, keep the rules and show you care, not for profit or for gain but for Oz's name. Aussies, Aussies, Aussies, Aussies, show that you are tried and true ones...'

I have been doing better collecting inspirational lines: 'Some old-fashioned things like fresh air and sunshine are hard to beat'. 'We do not know that the future holds, but we do know who holds the future.'

Here in the Parkville precinct, with eight other Jesuits (two lawyers, two other Anglos, one Chinese, and three Vietnamese, one of whom is a medical doctor), I have seen over six months of restricted living in our plague city slip by. One Anglo member of the community who normally spends part of a weekend in a very busy parish in the Western suburbs confessed that he has been feeling imprisoned. That prompted a big smile from one of the Vietnamese. After the fall of Saigon, having belonged to the elite South Vietnamese marine corps, he spent three years in a concentration camp before escaping on a boat. 'In the camp', he recalled, 'they shouted at you, went in for torture, and kept you at forced labour. The food was terrible and, if you played soccer against the guards, you had to make sure you lost. That's what it can mean to be imprisoned.'

Outside my kitchen, the red-flowering camellia has been a blaze of blooms, the best I have seen it in ten years. Since camellias were called after a Jesuit botanist (Georg Joseph Kamel) and flourish in Vietnam and China, our specimen may be registering its approval of the presence of the Vietnamese and Chinese Jesuits here on Royal Parade.

Viele Gruesse, Gerald.

August 2020.

[A round robin to relatives and friends.]

Life in plague-town has done wonders for my writing. I have been inspired by the example of the Russian Alexander Pushkin (holed up in the countryside during a cholera epidemic and coming up with *Eugene Onegin*) and the Italian Giovanni Boccaccio, faced with the black death but producing his best work. Maybe it's not my best but I have put together 18 articles (that I have published over nearly fifty years) on the Gospels, the Acts of the Apostles and themes of St Paul. The concluding chapter tells the story of how an article published in 1971 (on Paul's notion of divine power made perfect in his human weakness (2 Corinthians 12:9-10)) was subsequently received, rejected, or modified by biblical scholars. One of these was a German who treated me better than I deserved, probably since I engaged with an overwhelmingly German squad in my article. This latest opus from me is now being assessed by an American publisher [Paulist Press].

Life in lock-downed Melbourne has also started me reading some of the personal letters of St Ignatius Loyola and continuing my reading of Julian Barnes. Why didn't I pick up those letters years ago? They provide exceptionally vivid insights into the life and thinking of the founder of the Jesuits. As the pandemic broke, I was well into Barnes's latest, a tour de force built around the life of surgeon, Samuel Pozzi, whose portrait by John Singer Sargent provides the title: *The Man in the Red Coat*. Among Pozzi's merits—but there were also some serious demerits—was his defence of Alfred Dreyfus, the victim of gross personal injustice. As a reviewer has noted, the Dreyfusard Paris of 1909 sounds uncannily like Melbourne in 2019. [The reviewer had in mind the public 'conspiracy' set on turning Cardinal George Pell into a scapegoat.] This book prompted me into seeing again the film based on Barnes's *A Sense of an Ending*, which might be summed up by a line from his older friend (only acquaintance?), Philip Larkin: 'what will survive of us is love'. Next I plunged into Barnes' account of the inner struggles of Shostakovich, *The Noise of Time*. I have long wondered why the Russian composer resisted until Stalin's death the pressure to join the Communist party, but only did so when a thaw came under Khrushchev. Barnes supplies a satisfying explanation. Incidentally, you are more than halfway through the book before you learn the reason for the title: 'art is the whisper of history, heard above the noise of time' (p. 91 in my paperback edition). Barnes returns to this language a little later: 'the music of our being…if it is strong and pure enough to drown out the noise of time, is transformed into the whisper of history' (p. 125).

Our state premier is continuing his practice of personifying Covid-19, saying that 'it is a silent enemy and a very cunning enemy." What would Virgil think of this practice? That's a question for Jim [Peters, a nephew] and myself as we continue to swop quotations from the Aeneid.

26 September 2020.

Liebe Nevie,

I hope all is going 'spring-fully' at the University of Sydney. Down here on Royal Parade, I ply myself with sayings from Pope Francis (e.g. 'faith is not a light which scatters all our darkness but a lamp which guides our steps') and the motto of Xavier Jesuit School Cambodia ('dare to dream of a brighter future'). I find that motto courageous and moving, especially after hearing from Jesuit friends who work in South-East Asia. They persistently picture Cambodia as the most difficult and dangerous mission in that part of the world,

During the mini-break that came just before the current extreme lock-down, a young couple were married in our chapel here at the Jesuit Theological College. They turned up the other day with their lasting thanks in the form of a largish bush. With the help of Ai, one of our Vietnamese, I planted the bush in the front garden, right outside 159 Royal Parade and facing the steady stream of students from Melbourne University and nurses (from the Royal Melbourne Hospital) who continue to make their masked way up and down Royal Parade.

Yesterday the department of theology and religious studies at the University of San Francisco held a memorial service for Dan Kendall, who served on the faculty there since 1979. Marion [Peters] stood in for me. She read what I wanted to say about Dan, my first doctoral student and one with whom I did a lot of publishing over the years.

Last Sunday evening I switched on the opening instalment of the next series of *Grantchester*—a choice of pure nostalgia since, while the young vicar is stationed a few miles out of Cambridge, most of the action takes place at the University and, specifically, at Newnham College (with both the victim and the killer being students there). Among alumnae of Newnham, Emma Thompson, Germaine Greer, and our cousin Jane Ellison would all have been tempted to extreme language if they happened to have seen this instalment. It's not that several students of St John's College came out better. But there was no need to rubbish Newnham in that way. I can't wait to catch up again.

Much love, Gerald.

29 September 2020.

Lieber Gerald,

Things are indeed going springfully here, although I don't get to enjoy it much. I am a bit under the pump at the moment, submitting essays and spending some evenings/weekends with my unit in Randwick counting stock and moving boxes. It's good to have some extra pocket money but it's hard work. Come next week I should have a car to get myself there and back (thankfully). Dad is sending his old one up on a transporter. How lucky I am! No more taking the bus.

I have been going on walks/runs down past the Glebe foreshore and watching the seagulls at dusk. Their squawking is a nice soundtrack to my push ups. It's a good break from the chaos of uni and all the construction as well. I wake up to leaf blowers and cranes every morning—not exactly picturesque. I am just taking things week by week, enjoying my time with my friends. We eat on the library balcony most evenings, and then go and study next door. The weather is still temperamental but often the nights are warm.

The bush sounds nice. I have taken to doing some windowsill gardening myself. I have been 'propagating' (stealing) plants from the Wesley College gardens and growing them out of empty honey jars in my bedroom. It's good to have a little side-project for those fifteen- minute windows between getting back from the library and going to dinner. You know what I mean? I'll take a look at *Grantchester*. I hear there is a new season of *The Crown* coming out soon, this time featuring a young Princess Diana.

My essay on foreign policy ended up being a bit of a mess; I submitted it last night with a sigh. If it turns out that it's not as bad as I think and I get a good mark, I will send it to you. Otherwise, maybe the next one will be better.

Viel Liebe, Nevie.

Preaching Christmas at the End of the Pandemic Year

[As the first year of COVID-19 ended, in a December 2020 article for The Pastoral Review (St Mary's University, Twickenham), I reflected on ways in which Calvary continues to cast its shadow over preaching the nativity.]

As the year ends when COVID-19 has ravaged the world personally and economically, the shadow of the cross falls across Christmas 2020. The suffering that millions have endured can make them more sensitive to the ways in which Calvary is already present at Christ's birth in Bethlehem. The nativity anticipates his death and, we should add, his resurrection.

Luke on the Nativity

Luke reports how the Christ Child was 'laid in a manger', a miserable feeding trough for animals, because Mary and Joseph could find 'no place' in the local inn (Luke 2:7). A little over a month later, when they visited the Temple, a holy old man took the Baby in his arms, blessed God, and announced a message of salvation for 'all peoples', 'a light for revelation to the Gentiles and for glory' to God's people, Israel. But Simeon also warned Mary that Jesus' life and work would meet hostility and persecution: 'this child is destined for the falling and rising of many in Israel, and to be a sign that will be opposed' (Luke 2:25–35). Right from the birth of Jesus, Luke brings together light and darkness, life and the shadows of death.

Luke's account of the nativity includes shepherds who were illuminated by divine glory and visited by an angel of the Lord, who brought them 'good news of great joy for all the peoples'—the birth of 'a Saviour who is Christ the Lord'. A vast heavenly army joined the angel of the Lord, praising God and saying: 'Glory to God in the highest heaven, and on earth peace among those whom he favours'. The shepherds hastened to see the Christ Child. Then they returned to their sheep, 'glorifying and praising God for all that they had heard and seen' (Luke 2:8–20).

The sign of the manger, mentioned three times by Luke (2:7, 12, 16), symbolizes the humble birth of the Saviour who would die on a cross and be laid in a tomb. But his birth also brings the revelation of divine glory and a heavenly liturgy, led by an angelic choir. That revelation and liturgy acclaim the 'peace' that God conveys and the human 'joy' it evokes. Luke subtly links the birth of the Christ Child with his final 'rebirth' in the resurrection. At the end two angels will attest God's hand at work in the resurrection (Luke 24:4–5). The disciples experience 'peace' (Luke 24:36) and 'joy' (Luke 24:32, 41). Like the shepherds, the disciples saw the Saviour; then they 'returned to Jerusalem with great joy, and were continually in the temple blessing God' (Luke 24:52).

Attentive readers of Luke's opening and closing chapters catch the ways in which he joins the nativity with the death and resurrection of Christ. Both the beginning and the end of this story include the shadow of death. But they also feature the gift of divine peace and the joy with which human beings praise and bless what God does in the story of Jesus.

Matthew on the Nativity

Through the figure of King Herod, Matthew obviously introduces the danger of a violent death that menaces the Christ Child. An old and paranoid tyrant fears that this newborn Child will threaten the power he wants to pass on to his own son. And so Herod orders the massacre of all the little boys aged two years and under who live in or around Bethlehem (Matthew 2:16–18). But the link that Matthew establishes between the nativity and the crucifixion goes beyond the killing of the holy innocents.

First, there is the *question* put by the Magi: 'Where is he who has been born the king of the Jews?' (Matthew 2:2). This question receives an extended answer at the end of the Gospel, when Jesus is condemned, mocked, and crucified as 'the king of the Jews' (Matthew 27:11, 29, 37, 42). In this sense, the birth of Jesus anticipates his death. That birth and death take place for the redemption of all people, Jews *and Gentiles* alike—a fact also suggested at the beginning and the end of Matthew's Gospel. At the beginning, the Magi, who are not Jews, arrive from the East with their gifts for the newborn Jesus. At the end, the Roman centurion and the other soldiers responsible for the crucifixion exclaim after the death of Jesus, 'truly this man was the Son of God' (Matthew 27:54).

Secondly, an *angel of the Lord* creates another link between the nativity and what happened at the end. Matthew's story of the birth of Jesus features an 'angel of the Lord', the heavenly agent responsible for saving the Holy Family. God also acts to warn and save the Magi, after Herod tries to trick them into revealing the identity and whereabouts of the Christ Child. Those who stand obediently with God (Mary, her Child, Joseph, and the Magi) seem utterly weak and defenceless against the power of a wicked tyrant. But God effortlessly transforms the situation and rescues them. The figure of the 'angel of the Lord', who also comes on the scene shortly before and after that rescue (Matthew 1:20–25; 2:19–20), turns up in Matthew's Gospel only here at the beginning and then at the end (Matthew 28:2–7).

In his Easter story, Matthew contrasts (a) Jesus' few friends, merely two women (Mary Magdalene and 'the other Mary', who witness the burial of Jesus and visit his grave on Easter Sunday), and (b) the violent forces of injustice, represented by a squad of soldiers set to guard the tomb (Matthew 27:61–28:15). Against the hostile powers of the world, personified by the soldiers, those who side with Jesus seem helpless. He is dead and buried. Nothing more can happen. His body is locked away and will quietly decay. But then through the magnificent 'angel of the Lord', God acts dramatically to vindicate Jesus and the two women. In a stroke of delicious irony, the soldiers themselves become like helpless corpses. They thought they were guarding a dead body. Now it is they who fall to the ground and become 'like dead men'. The friends of God, the two holy women, may feel themselves to be helplessly weak and opposed by overwhelming might. But God changes everything and proves victorious over evil. This theme at the end of Matthew's Gospel recalls a central theme in the nativity story.

Christian Artists and the Nativity

In a painting attributed to a fifteenth-century artist, Benedetto Bonfigli, and exhibited in the National Gallery (London), the adoration of the Magi has been dramatically juxtaposed with a scene of the crucifixion. The direct juxtaposition of the two episodes, one from the beginning and the other from the end of Christ's earthly story, expresses the way in which he was born in order to die for humanity (represented by the Magi). In Bonfigli's work, the Infant Christ sits on a cushion placed on his Mother's lap and shows authority as he accepts the gifts of the three Magi. They are pictured as kings. The eldest of them has laid his crown on the ground and is holding the Child's feet—perhaps intending to kiss them with reverent submission. Acceptance of this homage is understood as Christ's acknowledging his suffering destiny. In fact, Bonfigli portrays the crucified Christ in the middle distance among some hills, his head bowed in death and blood dripping from his wounds.

In Luke's nativity narrative, the swaddling clothes symbolize the ordinary, human condition of the new born Christ Child. Like any baby he is wrapped in cloth bands. A few Western artists link these swaddling clothes of the Christ Child with the *loin cloth* he will wear on the cross. Thus on the Isenheimer altar painted by Mathias Grünewald (d. 1528), which includes a portrayal of Christmas, Our Lady holds her Child in the same cloth that Grünewald shows him wearing at the end of his life on the cross.

Sometimes, as is the case with 'The Mystical Nativity' (now in the National Gallery, London) by Sandro Botticelli (d. 1510), the swaddling clothes are associated with the *shroud* in which he will be buried. But Botticelli does more than associate the cross with the cave where Jesus was born and the manger in which he was laid. He introduces twelve angels dancing under the golden dome of heaven right above the Christ Child who is lying on a sheet in his rustic manger. Botticelli's masterpiece blends earthly poverty and lowliness with heavenly joy and celebration, the cross with the glory of risen life.

Geertgen Tot Sint Jans (d. about 1490) does not use either Christ's loin cloth or his shroud to link his birth with the crucifixion. In the 'Nativity at Night' (found in the National Gallery, London), the child lies completely naked in a rough and hard container. His future suffering can also be detected in the way Geertgen encloses the composition with the wooden beams of a stable. On the one hand, the beams show us that the child, if naked, is protected by a roof. On the other hand, the way the beams extend into the sky hints at the wooden arms of the cross on which the Christ Child will die for us.

The subtly tragic meaning of Geertgen's work is increased by the way in which he has rendered the manger with uncompromising toughness. It is more a coffin than a cradle. In front of the manger, some stalks of wheat allude to the fact that the Christ Child has come not only as the Light of the world (John 1:9) but also as the Bread of life (John 6), made available to everyone through his crucifixion and resurrection.

'The Adoration of the Kings' by Pieter Bruegel the Elder (d. 1569), also in the National Gallery, London, links (a) the visit of the Magi to the Christ Child with (b) the death that he would suffer on the cross for all human beings. The Baby is very small and almost naked, unlike the well clothed and heavily armed people who are standing nearby. The Child is afraid and shrinks back into the arms of his Mother. The piece of cloth which loosely covers him looks like a tiny shroud. He seems threatened by the weapons that the soldiers carry. The halberds of at least two of them suggest the form of a cross. One of the Magi offers the Child the gift of myrrh, an aromatic gum resin which was used in the Middle East to anoint corpses and which obviously refers to Christ's death and burial. The Child does not want to accept this gift, and we think naturally of the agonized struggle in the Garden of Gethsemane: 'Abba,

Father, everything is possible for you. Take this chalice away from me' (Mark 14:36). Bruegel apparently also wants to show the failure of many people to recognize their Saviour at the beginning of his story, as will happen at the end. In the painting, few look at the Child and some seem amazed at the rich gifts.

Christian Poets and the Nativity

Numerous Christian poets acknowledge the bond between Bethlehem and Calvary. Let me cite four of them.

First, St Robert Southwell (d. 1595) in his poem 'The Burning Babe' describes a vision he had on 25 December. 'A pretty Babe all burning bright' tells of his desire to wash sinners in his blood and purify them through the fire of his love. The poet repeatedly uses 'fire', 'blood', and 'love' to express the purpose of the nativity: the redemption of all human beings through Christ's death (and resurrection).

My second example is drawn from a major poet, John Dunne (d. 1631), but comes from a sermon he preached on Christmas Day. Donne pictures Christmas and Good Friday as so closely connected that they form one day: 'The whole life of Christ was a continual passion...His birth and death were but one continual act, and his Christmas Day and Good Friday are but the evening and the morning of one and the same day.'

Third, in a long poem, 'On the Morning of Christ's Nativity', John Milton concentrates on the paradox of God being born as an infant, the Creator who has become a baby. He also introduces a reference to the saving passion of Christ that is to come: 'The Babe lies yet in smiling infancy/That on the bitter cross/Must redeem our loss' (verse 16).

Fourth, in 1922 T. S. Eliot (d. 1965) published 'The Waste Land', a poem which was quickly recognised as one of the landmark works of modern poetry and which evoked the collapse of classical culture and humanism. In 1943 Eliot's 'The Four Quartets' revealed 'the end of all our exploring', a luminous and relatively peaceful reply to the anxious questions of 'The Waste Land'. Between the publication of the two works, Eliot had been received into the Anglican Church in 1927, the year in which he published 'The Journey of the Magi'.

In that poem the Magi, after a hard and long journey, succeed in finding the Christ Child and return home wondering: 'Were we led all that way for/Birth or Death?' Such details in the account of their journey as 'three trees on a low sky' have already alerted readers to the death Christ would suffer on a cross, flanked by two criminals on two other crosses. Eliot tells the story from the point of view of the Magi, but he joins Southwell, Donne, and Milton in acknowledging the profound link between the birth of Christ and the 'hard and bitter agony' of his death.

Conclusion

Like Luke and Matthew, Christian artists and poets have let us glimpse the deep connection between the birth of our Saviour and the end of his human history at the crucifixion and resurrection. Some sacred music also let us sense the profound union between Bethlehem and Calvary.

Many of those who hear 'The Passion according to St Matthew' are moved by the way Johann Sebastian Bach (d. 1750) incorporated a hymn by Paul Gerhardt (d. 1676), namely 'O Haupt voll Blut und Wunden' ('O Sacred Head Sore Wounded' in the translation by Robert Bridges). But they may not all be aware that Bach also embodied something from this same hymn at the beginning of his 'Christmas Oratorio'. The great composer sensed the connection between the nativity and the death of Christ.

At Christmas 2020, preachers and catechists will feel the need to reflect on the painfully new ways in which millions of human beings, through the impact of COVID-19, have shared in the passion of Jesus and continue to do so. The inspired writers of the New Testament, along with Christian artists, poets, and composers offer rich insights and images to fill out the links between Bethlehem and Calvary that have been played out once again in our world.

4

Letters from January 2021 to June 2021

16 January 2021.

[To a German married couple, Bernhard and Steffi Graf, medical doctors of Regensburg, who spent time with me years before in Milwaukee, USA. Bernhard's brother, now Bishop Josef Graf, wrote his doctoral thesis under my direction at the Gregorian University.]

Dear Steffi and Bernhard,

Every blessing for 2021 to you, to Mini and Max, and to all your dear ones, and thanks for the news. You have held your heads high in a fiercely demanding time. I am very pleased M. and M. are doing so well.

A month ago, I was discharged from a Melbourne hospital (Epworth) after 35 days battling a thyroid gland that had run amok and was causing heart problems. Now I face the daily grind of rehabilitation exercises, as they call them.

Last summer Paulist Press (Mahwah, New Jersey) published my co-authored *Jesuits, Theology and the American Catholic Church*. In early

2022 they will put out *Illuminating the New Testament: the Gospels, Acts and Paul.*

After a year of lockdown, it is hard to imagine what our post-vaccine world will look like. *Vorsicht*—what is the best English or Italian equivalent?— has been the reigning slogan. Still 'caution'?

Many thanks for the perennial friendship you have shown me. I remain most grateful and pray for you and all your dear ones. I will be at Campion House, 99 Studley Park Road, Kew, Victoria 3101, until early February. Then, all going well, I move back to the Jesuit Theological College, 175 Royal Parade, Parkville, Victoria 3052, where I normally reside. Google 'Kew' and 'Parkville' (both 'Australia') and you will see they are not very distant.

Peace, love and good cheer, Gerald.

6 March 2021.

[To Brett O'Neill, an Australian Jesuit studying for his doctorate at Boston College. As Brett had recently belonged to my community, I filled him in briefly about the sayings and doings of the Jesuits still there: Anglos, several Vietnamese, and one Chinese]

Dear Brett,

I was delighted to learn that you had been vaccinated and will shortly receive a second shot. We are still in the waiting mode here, but my sleeve is ready to be rolled up asap.

I do hope one or more journals have the good sense to accept your papers for publication. That is a great idea to submit them. You always had something valuable to say, and now even more so in the course of your doctoral studies.

Every now and then my past catches up with me. Sometimes that takes the form of a person who has not been in touch for many years dropping me a line or sending me an e-mail. This week the return to the past involved a lady called Aisling, who has worked over twenty years in New York City for an association, the Xavier Society for the Blind, which serves a pool of 500,000 people and does so by recording books and/or publishing them in braille. They have recorded a book I published back in 1983, *Finding Jesus* (Paulist Press), and let me know that it was the seventh most requested in February. At the time this study of John's Gospel as a guide for Lent, a collection of articles I had published on John for *America* magazine, pleased me and sold well. But the book has long dropped out of sight. I hope the Xavier Society follows up its foray into my past by choosing other books of mine for translation. It is encouraging to learn of serving the disabled on the other side of the globe.

Paulist Press, by the way, early next year will publish a collection of my biblical essays, *Illuminating the New Testament: the Gospels, Acts and Paul*. I have been collecting names for back cover endorsements, and the Paulist Press seems satisfied with my team: Brendan Byrne, Nicholas King, Dorothy Lee, and Ronald Witherup. I hold Sarah Coakley and Tom Wright in reserve.

This morning I went over from Royal Parade for my first coffee on Lygon Street, which is once again full of Saturday morning buzz. Ai was off to say a Mass on the third anniversary of a friend's death from lung cancer. Right now (Saturday afternoon) Hoa is running a session of prayer and reflection for nine leaders of Vietnamese CLC [Christian Life Communities]. Brendan has left for his Saturday evening Mass in Hopper's Crossing. Justin and I will eat after six when the Vietnamese send us food in the common room. Our Chinese Jesuit student, Andrew, is presumably out ministering in Box Hill to the spiritual needs of his compatriots. We await the return of Steve (from Amman, Jordan), Minh-Uoc (from Adelaide, South Australia), and Jamie Calder (from Perth, Western Australia). With Cao (still flourishing as spiritual father at the Melbourne diocesan seminary), we make up a community of ten.

Every spiritual and academic blessing as you move into spring, Gerry.

4 April 2021.

[A letter to my niece Victoria ('Tori') O'Collins, who lives with her three children in Singapore. I speak about her cousin, Lizzie Peters who lives in Melbourne and has just given birth to a boy, the first grandchild of Justin and Jill Peters.]

Dearest Tori,

The arrival of Xander is giving my family much joy: Lizzie had the baby at home (with the help of a midwife).

Whatever else lockdowns against COVID-19 have achieved, they seemed to have made truck drivers more resolutely courteous. In the last couple of weeks, the drivers of two huge vehicles stopped to wave me across the road. In the first case, I could easily and happily have waited; in the other case, I was in fact waiting for a red light to turn green; in both cases, there was no danger to me whatsoever. The giant trucks filled their half of the road and left no room for any cars to buzz by on either side.

After my thyroid ran amok and gave me 35 days in a hospital and over 60 days in a Jesuit retirement centre in Kew, I was very happy to return to Parkville and the Jesuit Theological College on 15 February. They have put me downstairs for the moment. To return to my old upstairs quarters, I continue to walk and exercise unfailingly. I hope to persuade the rest of the Jesuit community that my medical specialist, Dr Walter Plehwe, a charming and learned endocrinologist in the twilight of his career, has agreed that my thyroid gland may have poisoned me for a while but it shouldn't stop me now from going back upstairs to live.

For the time being I potter along writing articles for a squad of journals, popular (*The Furrow*, *The Pastoral Review*, and *The Tablet*) and professional (*The Australian Biblical Review*, *Colloquium*, *The Expository Times*, *New Blackfriars*, *The Scottish Journal of Theology*, *The Way*, and *Worship*). Two books are moving down the pipeline: *Illuminating the New Testament: The Gospels, Acts, and Paul* (Mahwah, NJ: Paulist Press) and *Letters From Rome and Beyond* (Brisbane: Connor Court Publishing). For the moment I am abstaining from climbing the heights of theology by attempting to write another (it would be my 79th) book. Your name turns up repeatedly in the index of *Letters from Rome and Beyond*.

As history slides into the past, a very blessed Easter to you, the three children, and all your friends. May the risen Jesus fill you with the joy that he shared with Mary Magdalene, Peter, and his other cherished friends,

Gerald.

'Does Hans Küng remain relevant?' [An article on Hans Küng commissioned by 'The Pastoral Review' in April 2021 and published 17/3 (July-September 2021), pp. 42–45.]

Major obituaries of Hans Küng (died 6 April 2021) have highlighted his astonishing gifts as a communicator—he spoke five European languages—along with his prodigious capacity for research and writing that produced around fifty books. The obituaries have evoked the flexibility that let him move from issues concerned with church reform and interchurch relations, to questions about Jesus Christ, the existence of God, eternal life, and, finally, the need for peace between religions and for the practice of a world ethic.

When Pope John XXIII announced in January 1959 his intention to convoke a general council, Küng responded with a best-selling work, The Council: Reform and Reunion (1960). He spelled out in a popular style the cry for reforms to purify the Catholic Church in the light of the gospel that had already come from such theological giants as Yves Congar.

During the four years of Vatican II (1962–65), Küng did much personally to publicize (and evaluate) the Council's proceedings. He also joined an American Jesuit, Daniel O'Hanlon, and Congar in preparing a volume of important speeches delivered at Vatican II. A tireless networker, he was—so Robert Kaiser, the Time magazine journalist at the Council, told me— 'always the last to leave the Sunday evening receptions given by my wife and myself in our Roman apartment'.

At a time when the majority of Christians made the theory and practice of church life their favored topic, Küng published two widely read studies: Structures of the Church (1962) and The Church (1967). He developed an historical approach, but without ever thinking through what that involved. Did it simply require taking an 'honest look' at the data, a view that he proposed on occasions and that the great Bernard Lonergan dismissed as insufficient? Whose version of history can we rely on? What role does the living tradition have for those who interpret historical records? Küng was undoubtedly sensitive to the questions coming from western culture and unbelief. But his answers sometimes seemed to sacrifice doctrinal orthodoxy and genuine historical research for the sake of contemporary relevance.

Küng's views of the Church triggered more debate by the way he chose to 'celebrate' a hundred years since papal primacy and infallibility were officially defined at the First Vatican Council in 1870. He questioned that teaching in *Infallible? An Enquiry* (German original, 1970). Philosophers, as well as theologians, became involved in a worldwide discussion. Küng's work raised questions about the nature of truth and infallible propositions. He did not always reach the standard of clarity that contemporary analytic philosophers required.

Many noticed how the book exaggerated the authoritative status of the papal rejection of 'artificial' birth control expressed in Paul VI's 1968 encyclical, *Humanae Vitae*. For the official presentation of the document, the Pope made sure that the monsignor involved made no claims that the encyclical offered infallible teaching. But such were the subsequent claims of some conservative commentators. It was easier for Küng to reject their arguments after he had accepted or at least implied that their exaggerated and unwarranted claims rightly recognized the exercise of papal infallibility.

The English translation of *Infallible* was available when he visited Melbourne in 1971 at the invitation of local Anglicans. They had been touched by his ecumenical gesture in dedicating *The Church* to the Archbishop of Canterbury, Michael Ramsey. It was Ramsey who in 1966 came to Rome for an historic meeting with Paul VI, which ended with the Pope giving Ramsey his own episcopal ring. Ramsey opened the Anglican Centre in Rome and made its director his personal representative to the Vatican. Ramsey also recommended *The Church* to the Anglican bishops preparing for the next Lambeth Conference. But it was Küng's latest book—rather than the earlier work dedicated to Archbishop Ramsey—that triggered wide public attention.

When Küng arrived at Melbourne airport, I walked out onto the tarmac to welcome him off the plane. None of his Anglican hosts had ever met him before. Our handshake set the stage for an Australian Broadcasting film, *Meet Hans Küng*. I encouraged my eldest sister Moira Peters to hold a cocktail party in his honour. The Catholic Archbishop of Melbourne, James (later Cardinal) Knox, pleaded a previous engagement and did not attend. The reception became an occasion for the handsome, charming, and stylishly dressed Swiss theologian to hold court.

Knox invited Küng to meet him a few days later. They exchanged gifts. Knox gave his visitor a book on Mother Teresa of Calcutta, and received from him a copy of *Infallible?* Küng's gift bore the message in Latin, '*non ad ecclesiam destruendam sed aedificandam* (not for destroying the Church but for building it up)'. He was utterly sincere in his deep desire to build up and bless the family of God that Jesus and his first followers had called into being.

I mention all this partly to set the record straight. In the second volume of his autobiography, *Disputed Truth* (German original, 2007), when Küng tells the story of his Melbourne visit, he changes my surname to 'O'Connor'. He also moves the reception I arranged from my sister's home in the city (Orrong Road, Toorak) out to her 'family estate', presumably in the countryside. He says nothing about his friendly meeting with Archbishop Knox. He complains about Catholics failing to join the Anglicans in inviting him to give five major lectures at the University of Melbourne, which drew up to one thousand people each evening.[3]

A week after Küng's visit to Melbourne, during a very well attended theological meeting held at the University of Sydney, I took as my subject 'the honest to infallibility' debate which Küng's latest book had prompted. He responded to my paper in his cheerful, self-assured way. He agreed that I had fairly reported the criticisms being made, and reiterated his positions. In the subsequent stages of the debate over his *Infallible?* book, he continued to insist that no one had shown that his challenge to papal infallibility needed any real correction, revision, or serious clarification.

I remained grateful that he pushed me into reflecting further on the Church, and fulfilling my responsibility towards her life and growth. Two years later, in 1973, Archbishop Knox staged a Eucharistic Congress in Melbourne. I was determined to work towards the goal of a truly international and ecumenical conference that would encourage the Christian churches in Australia to seek unity more effectively.

I invited Jürgen Moltmann, now celebrated for his theology of hope and theology of the cross, to stay with me at the Jesuit Theological College in Parkville, an inner suburb of Melbourne. One evening in the Melbourne Town Hall, he joined Mother Teresa of Calcutta and spoke to three thousand people on our Christian vocation to spread peace. He teased me afterwards: 'Is that what you wanted to do at the Eucharistic Congress? Make a team out of Catholic saint

---

[3] *Disputed Truth: Memoirs*, trans. John Bowden (London: Continuum, 2008), 199.

and a leading Protestant theologian?' 'Jürgen', I pointed out, 'that's a winning formula—you on the theory of peace and Mother Teresa on the practice of peace'.

To return to Küng's visit to Sydney in 1971. During a TV interview when asked by an ex-Catholic, 'are you trying to rock the boat of Peter?', Küng responded: 'No, I'm only trying to help people love Jesus more'. The day after this TV appearance his car stopped at a traffic light en route to a boat trip around Sydney harbor. The driver of another car pulled alongside, rolled down his window, and said: 'I saw you on television last night. You're Hans Küng, aren't you?' 'Yes', said Küng. 'Did you agree with me?' 'Yes, about fifty per cent.' 'Great', replied Küng. 'you're half way there already'. He meant, I believe, 'half way there in finding love for Jesus'.

With his book on infallibility signalling the end of his first stage of writing (on church matters), Küng turned to questions about Jesus, who he was and is, and what he has done and continues to do for us. A long section on Jesus appeared at the heart of his remarkably successful *On Being a Christian* (German original, 1974). From the point of view of professional theology, it was no match for the Christology of Walter Kasper that appeared in the same year, *Jesus the Christ*. Küng re-ran a discredited view that had criticized the early church councils as fatally 'hellenizing' the gospel account of Jesus. He downplayed the full status and meaning of the virginal conception and bodily resurrection, and put the German bishops' teeth on edge by lack of clarity over the divine identity of Jesus. Nevertheless, the warmly affectionate portrait of Jesus produced by Küng proved effective in winning or winning back disciples for Jesus. Speaking on Vatican Radio, the Cardinal Archbishop of Vienna, Frans König, reported that, in his experience, *On Being a Christian* had already brought a thousand people back to the practice of faith in Christ.

From reflection on Jesus, Küng moved to questions of God. His 1978 book *Does God Exist? An Answer for Today* raised questions out of the historical situation of our time and (western) culture. 'We may really begin to wonder if Christianity has come to an end? Is it all over with belief in God? Has religion any future? Can we have morality even without religion? Is science sufficient? Has religion developed out of magic? Will it perish in the process of evolution? Is God from the outset a projection of human beings (Feuerbach), an opium of the people (Marx), and an illusion of those who have remained infantile (Freud)?'

But 'like everything connected with atheism and nihilism', Küng argued, 'it [dying into nothingness] cannot be refuted, but neither can it be positively proved. There never has been anyone who proved that we die into nothingness.' He claimed 'an absolutely reasonable, enlightened trust. It seems more reasonable, it seems reasonable every time, that I should die not into nothingness but into God.'

Turning in his fifties to write in a popular style about interreligious dialogue (*Christianity and the World Religions: Paths of Dialogue with Islam, Hinduism and Buddhism*, 1986), Küng exposed himself to criticisms coming from experts on those religions. When writing about Hinduism, he lacked the depth of scholarship and lifelong experience deployed by Jacques Dupuis (*Toward a Christian Theology of Religious Pluralism*, 1997). When Dupuis (whom I called 'Jim') came under fire in 1998 from the Congregation for the Doctrine of the Faith, Küng contacted him and offered support. 'Thank him, Jim', I advised, 'but decline help. His help might cause unnecessary trouble. You have a strong case anyway.'

Nevertheless, only the obtuse could argue with Küng's much-quoted conclusion: 'No peace among nations without peace among the religions. No peace among the religions without dialogue between the religions. No dialogue between the religions without investigation of the foundation of the religions' (*Christianity: Essence, History, Future*, 1995).

At the Parliament of the World Religions held in Chicago in 1993, Küng was mainly responsible for drafting *Towards a Global Ethic: An Initial Declaration.* When the Parliament of the World Religions met in Melbourne in 2009, he drew a limited audience and little media attention. He put this down to the Catholic Church working against him. Others thought of what Moltmann, his Protestant colleague in Tübingen, had said in warning years before when a leading German magazine (*Der Spiegel*) turned against Küng and his self-assured declarations: 'don't base your life and success on the media'. Using the English language for its front cover, the magazine had editorialized, 'The King Can Do No Wrong'.

Several obituaries that appeared after Küng's death last April quoted a classic criticism of his readiness to pontificate for the media on any manner of questions: 'he could never be pope because he would lose his infallibility' (e.g. the London *Times*, 8 April). In a profound understatement the *Telegraph* remarked: 'he was opinionated and talkative, which some found tiresome' (8 April). Years ago his contemporary theologian, Johann Baptist Metz, confessed that he couldn't accept two *magisteria* (the Church's and Küng's): 'sometimes', he quipped, 'I find even one *magisterium* too much'.

For years Küng displayed the less than endearing habit of presenting himself as *the* champion of truth and genuine Christian freedom. Those who differed from him were dismissed as envious, ambitious, and lacking honesty. His criticisms of popes tended to being unnuanced and intemperate—to put it mildly. At a dinner given by Priscilla Collins (of William Collins publishing) in her London home, he raged against Paul VI to the point that another (very distinguished) guest invited by Lady Collins, Henry Chadwick, told him bluntly: 'Hans, would you please shut up'. William Collins published the English translations of *On Being a Christian*, *Does God Exist?*, and other works by Küng.

When Giuseppe Alberigo, editor of a five-volume study of Vatican II, accurately presented Küng as only a minor contributor to the Council, Küng accused him of being a 'court theologian'. It was a ridiculous charge against an independent-minded, lay professor at the University of Bologna who took his distance from Vatican officials and was ignorantly criticized by them.

Along with such personal limits and flaws, one should recognize the effective, apologetic nature of much of Küng's writing. He never reached the theological depth of Congar or Rahner. Nevertheless, he made a valuable contribution not only to preparing for the Second Vatican Council and spreading its teachings and reforms but also, years later, to interreligious dialogue and relations. Even more importantly, he showed how his radical questioning co-existed with faith in God and a deep love for Jesus, who with his apostolic followers founded the Church. In his own (admittedly polemical) way, Küng was and remained a powerful witness to a living faith in God and Catholic Christianity.

4 May 2021.

Lieber Gerald,

Hello from Sydney! It's our first official rainy day of the year. Luckily I can do my classes from zoom if I want to. I undertook an Arabic quiz just now from my desk. I am starting to feel the speed pick-up with my Arabic, a feeling I'm sure you're familiar with. Very motivating.

I am giving a presentation in French this week about recent events in Burundi. We have to talk about a recent piece of news in '*le monde francophone*', and I thought I would think outside of the box and discuss Africa. Wish me luck!

Doing only three subjects is a blessing. I'm enjoying going on walks to the foreshore, sitting around at lunch with my friends, and reading books in the afternoon. The army and the German society keep me busy, though. Our Monday and Wednesday conversation groups are going crazy! Not the Monday ones (on zoom) so much— usually we get only one or two people who attend. But Wednesdays are great fun. I think it's a special type of person who decides to put an hour of their day away to sit down at a café and discuss their life in German with a bunch of strangers. Language is such an equalizer in that way—nothing like a grammatical blunder to bring everyone down to the same level.

We had an army weekend this weekend where we did some programming of radios. It was nice to see my friends and learn some new skills. Still thinking about applying to be an officer, but I need to prove myself first; so I'll keep showing up, I guess.

I am also enjoying my little, one-hour a week politics tutoring stint at Wesley. It's a great way to meet other students and hear what they think of college life. Except I was accidentally logging half-hour lunch breaks on the new app they use to pay us, so I got paid only half for last week. I was a bit of an awkward conversation with the Finance Manager (Jenny) the other day, but she was very helpful and nice, so that's a win.

I hope all is well in Parkville. I wish I could pop around to catch up with you for bowl of pasta. Hopefully I will be back in Melbourne soon. Annie's 21st [Annie Coleman] is coming up on 21 May and I should be around Thursday to Sunday, but no flights booked yet. Tell me all the news!

Lots of love, Nevie.

8 May 2021.

[To Monica Ellison, a cousin who lived in Wimbledon, UK.]

Dearest Monica,

a very happy and blessed birthday tomorrow. For some months now my Jesuit community has included a priest from northern China who is engaged with securing a master's degree in spirituality. Finally, he decided to take a break from reading and writing; incessant essays are the heart of the course. Last week Andrew Zhao thought it was about time he connected with Australian wildlife and drove himself up to Hanging Rock, around 40 minutes to the north of Melbourne. Kangaroos 'a-abounded' and he even caught sight of a koala bear. Over the evening meal he was poised to accept as history *Picnic at Hanging Rock*. We had to insist on the fictional status of the book and the film. [It is a story of city school girls on picnic, one or two of whom disappear mysteriously.]

Last week I received my first anti-COVID-19 jab, and did so in the Melbourne Exhibition Building, an architectural icon built in 1880 where I faced examinations as a schoolboy. It must have been the first time I stepped into the vast building since 1948.

In an hour or so, Melissa or someone else from the Royal Melbourne Hospital rehabilitation will arrive to check whether I am doing my exercises and possibly teach me one or two new tricks. But for the moment they may have to be cautious. Yesterday David Clarke, a urologist who trained with my brother Jim, did a little probing to establish that a stricture is causing a problem. Is 'stricture' the correct word? At least there is something 're-stricting' flow, and David is poised to deal with it in a few days.

Our lovely cook-manager (Annie) is shedding a few tears these days. A heart attack carried off her beautiful dog. 'We will get our beloved dogs back in heaven', I assured her. Every best and affectionate wish for the summer,

Gerald.

21 May 2021.

[To Laura Zampetti, whom I came to know as a school girl in the 1970s when she lived at Albano Laziale, outside Rome. For years she has been working for the European Union, and has now been moved to Podgorica, the capital of Montenegro.]

Carissima, buon compleanno (happy birthday), ad multos annos. I hope/pray you have avoided our common foe, COVID-19. Australia has escaped, largely by becoming isolated. Yesterday my grand-niece, Genevieve (Nevie) Peters (daughter of Jim, with the flaming red hair) dropped in for lunch. She was down briefly from the University of Sydney, where she has been studying French, German and Arabic) for three years. She intends to move on to a career in the foreign service and has received, I think, a federal government scholarship to prepare for that work.

My sister Maev continues to live in Canberra, an hour's flight from Melbourne. We are the only two survivors of three girls and three boys. Maev and I have to be content to talk on the phone—two or three times a week.

I hope all goes very well for you, wherever you are currently living. An Australia-size hug, Gerald.

24 May 2021

My dear Gerald,

thank you for remembering the date of my birthday. I have so far escaped, and got the two shots of Pfizer between April and early May. Feeling a bit reassured, I dared to fly to Rome last Friday. I had a long, nice day in Rome yesterday. I also walked in the Piazza dei Santi Apostoli, where I recalled your observation on that pope's [Clement XIV, who supressed the Jesuit order in 1773] tomb being lower than the Gregorian's building.

I went for a few moments to the via delle Vergini to visit Saint

Rita's chapel. I will be in Italy until 5 June, also for my medical check-ups, and then back to Brussels. Early September I will move to Podgorica, for a new job (and house) there. Glad to hear that you are fine, and that part of the family is around. Un grande abbraccio (a big hug), Laura.

5
Letters from July 2021 to December 2021

27 July 2021.

[Sister Nuria Calduch Benages studied at the Biblical Institute, and began teaching at the Gregorian University in 1991, after I invited her to lead a seminar on the Old Testament.]

Dear Nuria,

I was absolutely delighted to read of your being nominated the secretary of the Pontifical Biblical Commission. *Le mie congratulazioni di cuore* (my heartfelt congratulations). You have done so much good, and this appointment will expand even further the good you already do. Sadly there is much 'bad news', but your appointment is part of the good news and something I found most encouraging.

These last few years I have turned more and more to writing biblical articles, and have, for example, published a number of articles with *The Expository Times* (Edinburgh). They have just accepted another article from me: on John 21:14 and its particular theological significance.

Di nuovo le mie congrazioni di cuore (once again my heartfelt congratulations). *Nel Signore risorto* (in the risen Lord), Gerald O'Collins, SJ.

29 July 2021.

[After my sister Maev died suddenly in Canberra on 3 July, it took time to bring the body to Melbourne and arrange the funeral Mass (at Newman College) and the burial (Kew cemetery). This is the homily I preached at the funeral].

These days, relatives, friends like Bishop Pat Power, and others have been sending me their personal tributes to Maev. One called her a 'remarkable, international scholar who did wonderful work in PNG. She did everything in capital letters'. Another wrote: 'Maev was a spectacular godmother. She made an enormous difference to my life over many decades.' Yet another wrote: 'I feel deeply sad. Such a wonderful woman. Such a wonderful family woman. Maev would say: "Just thinking about you; so I decided to give you a call."' Professor Patrick McArdle described her as 'a champion for vulnerable people, a person of extraordinary warmth, welcome, and conscience.' One of her nephews put it this way: 'Maev embraced life with open arms. She transformed the mundane into the magical and the everyday into a great adventure.'

Yet another nephew summed up the values Maev lived by: 'she spent a lifetime persistently and patiently bringing down barriers and merely human doctrines that have imprisoned peoples and cultures. Maev always challenged us to open our minds to the reality of beautifully diverse ways, and to the power of faith to shape the future.'

One academic colleague spoke of Maev's bright eyes and beautiful smile. Another academic colleague had this to say in a letter: 'Maev was indeed a great teacher whose kindness and compassion given to her students, regardless of who they were and where they came from, were boundless. May her beautiful soul be remembered forever and ever.'

Maev passed away quietly at home—just as she would have wanted it. She died, it seems, reading the newspaper. One person commented: 'the news is so awful; it can kill you'. But we might also recall the way Maev kept very much in touch with the real news around her and with the deep needs of the people wherever she lived.

There were some years when she was in New York, studying at Columbia University and then teaching at Hunter College. I was a visiting professor within the Boston Theological Institute. Yes, she did come up to visit me in Cambridge, Massachusetts. But she much preferred me to fly down and spend time with her in New York where I could support her various causes. One weekend she helped welcome a delegation of five Australian aborigines, Jack Davis and four others, visiting the United Nations. Another weekend, during the campaign against the war in Vietnam, the FBI raided her church and arrested Philip Berrigan, the brother of Dan Berrigan. When she had free time, Maev would pop over to nearby Harlem and take African American boys and girls out for some project or celebration.

Maev never wavered in the practice of her faith, and it was a thoroughly practical faith. I have never known a Christian who practised more faithfully what St James wrote in his letter: 'faith without works is dead'. Working for others was the heart of Maev's life. Often what she did for others belonged to the ordinary tasks of her life. But sometimes she was faced with a tragic emergency that Jesus describes in his parable of the Good Samaritan: some wounded, half-dead person lying on the side of her road. She never hesitated about stepping in like a good Samaritan.

Jesus left us the challenge of his extraordinary parable: the Good Samaritan. Jesus also left us a promise that belongs to Maev if it belongs to anyone: 'I will come again and take you to myself, so that where I am you also may be.' Jesus has taken Maev to himself and is surely sharing with her the company of the nephew she loved so well, Dominic. The good, loving Lord had seen to it that Maev died on the anniversary of Dominic's death.

With Maev's death, a great light has gone out of our lives. May she rest in peace and rise in glory. As well as anyone, St Augustine sums up for us the place to which Maev has gone.

All shall be Amen and Alleluia. We shall rest and we shall see.

We shall see and we shall know. We shall know and we shall love.

We shall love and we shall praise. Behold our end which is no end.

10 August 2021.

[A letter to two nieces, Victoria O'Collins and Ellie O'Collins.]

Dearest Tori and Ellie,

a loving 'Hi' from lock-downed Parkville. Our state premier talks about being 'gutted'. But what about us? If we didn't have the Olympic Games to watch, we might have risen in a desperate, hopeless revolution.

On Wednesday last, just before we were all confined to our homes, a friend, Michael Bartlett, invited me to a lecture on the origin of wine in (surprise, surprise) the country of Georgia—a lecture delivered with very well chosen slides during lunch at the

Australian Club (William Street). Several archeologists from the University of Melbourne have done digs in Georgia and uncovered the earliest evidence for wine making and wine consumption. Maybe others will dig up evidence showing that human beings were producing and drinking the stuff elsewhere and earlier. But right now the ancient inhabitants of Georgia are leading the rush for the gold medal.

On Tuesday of last week Denis White who produces wonderful oil hosted me for lunch at the Melbourne Club and, as always, brought along a bottle of olive oil for the toast I indulge at breakfast. Denis used to be office manager for Malcolm Fraser. He is a close friend of David Kemp, who is just about to finish publishing a five-volume history of Australian liberalism. That should produce a long delayed, alternate reading of Oz history to replace that of Manning Clark. Google 'Clark' and you will see what I mean,

Writing articles on New Testament topics for journals like *The Expository Times*—Robert Murray, SJ, used to call it disrespectfully *The Suppository Times*—keeps my mind off the pandemic. Some articles are directly positive: why e.g. does Matthew's Gospel repeatedly use the name of Jesus in his final resurrection chapter? The themes of other articles are a bit negative: what, for instance, is wrong with the thesis of Philippians 2:6-11 being an example of Angel Christology? I find the thesis quite implausible, not least because Paul has little time for angels.

Google 'Rock Lodge', our old family home in what is now called Frankston South, and the estate agent will give you a romantic, gilded view of the place where we grew up.

Much love, Gerald

16 August 2021.

[From my cousin Monica in Wimbledon.]

My dear Gerald, Thank you for letting me know about Maev. She was one, big, unforgettable personality and I feel fortunate to have met her. I was always interested in Maev's adventures in Papua, since my first ever job in publishing was contacting Erik de Mauny who with his first wife translated a book called *Mitsinari: Twenty Years amongst the Papuans of New Guinea*.

I later got to know Erik well when he was BBC correspondent in Paris—in fact so well that I was witness to his second wedding to Liz Strickland, who was Catholic. She decided that, since I knew when to stand up and kneel down at the Mass, I should be her 'maid of honour'. I never knew how Liz pulled that one off with the Vatican! [It's] intriguing how little connections circle and roost.

The world gets more dire by the day. I feel we had it good, days travelled without guilt or fear—in my case even to the border of Afghanistan. [At one stage Monica worked in Pakistan for a pipe-laying company.] Fat chance of that now. Lucky to be still on chemotherapy.

With much love, and keep the prayers coming, Monica.

[When she wrote, Monica was suffering from a terminal cancer, which carried her off just before Christmas. In January her son-in-law, Richard Tait, delivered the following eulogy at the funeral Mass in the parish church of Wimbledon.]

Eulogy for Monica Ellison

The great historian of the French revolution Richard Cobb talked of the richness of the lives of people who had a 'second identity'—in his case he felt both British and French. Monica went one step further—she had three identities—Irish, French and British. All three enriched her life and those of all who had the great good fortune to know her.

First, Ireland. Monica O'Connor was born in Wexford. Irish culture and history were important to her throughout her life. It is great to see the family from Ireland represented here and watching from their homes and to have heard Janet's wonderful music [her niece playing the Irish harp]. Monica was proud of her family's links with the struggle for Irish independence in the nineteenth century—among the family heirlooms, they preserved the chair they brought out for its heroes—Daniel O'Connell, the Liberator, who won catholic emancipation, and Charles Stuart Parnell, who so nearly achieved home rule—to be offered to the great men when they came to hold mass meetings. They also had close links with Britain—Monica's father, a dentist, was a medical officer in the British Army in the first world war and sent Monica to school in England.

Her love of Ireland and sense of Irish identity never left her—Monica's last history project was about Ireland—to encourage us to research a second family heirloom—the letter she displayed in her flat from Daniel O'Connell himself, who was in prison at the time. We found it was addressed to one of a quite large number of young female admirers visiting him and in this case the young woman was asking for his autograph. Monica was very amused to discover that even in his 70s and put in gaol by the British, the Liberator was still spending his time and thoughts with the ladies.

Monica was clever, cultivated and beautiful—she worked first in publishing in London, where she had an eye for talent and innovative writing, and then joined Aer Lingus as cabin crew, in the exciting and pioneering days of post-war air travel. Then, at the Wexford Opera Festival, she met John Ellison, a young and ambitious reporter who was to become one of the great foreign correspondents of the golden age of Fleet Street. Theirs was a loving marriage of two strong minded and independent personalities—a partnership which was the rock on which they built their lives. They enjoyed so much together —the cut and thrust of European (and Fleet Street) politics, travelling the world, walking together in beautiful countryside, from the Mediterranean to the Surrey

Letters from July 2021 to December 2021

Hills, and bringing up their family.

John was appointed Paris Bureau Chief of the *Daily Express*—a huge job, covering Europe, the Middle East and Africa and bringing a second identity—France. Monica set up home for John and their four daughters in the French capital. There was a flat in the smart *seizième arrondissement*, a *maison de campagne* in the Ardèche. There were French friends and international friends. Everyone was welcomed with warmth and kindness. On Boxing Day she organised a car treasure hunt round Paris with riddles and clues and food and drink at the end. When the 1968 riots broke out, the Ellison flat was the rendezvous for journalists setting out to cover them— Monica drove them to the Left Bank with string vests chopped up as makeshift gas masks. Jane, Juliet, Emma and Charlotte all went into the French school system—Monica became an expert on the poets and writers of the French curriculum.

On one occasion, Monica's kindness was nearly her undoing. One summer in the Ardèche, the family were adopted by a friendly and apparently abandoned cat who wandered into their house. Holidays over, Monica agreed to take the little animal back to Paris, where she had him neutered and he spent a happy year as the family pet. The next summer back to the Ardèche for *les vacances*. The cat disappeared as suddenly as he had turned up. A few days later an encounter with the mayor of the village solved the mystery— lovely to see you, he said, by the way we're celebrating the return of our beloved little cat— he went missing this time last year and we thought he'd been stolen and gone for ever but he's back—he's clearly been well looked after—however there is a mystery—he's not quite as he was—someone has had him '*castré*' if you know what I mean, Madame Ellison. Of course, Madame Ellison *did* know but wasn't going to let on how it had happened.

When John's career took him away from Paris to New York and then London, that could have been the end of the French identity—but far from it. Three of her bi-lingual daughters made their lives in France and brought up their families there. There were gatherings in Wimbledon and visits and holidays in beautiful parts of France - the Beaujolais, the Atlantic coast, the Ile de France, the Alps. Monica was always there for her children and her grandchildren with love, advice and help when they needed it. She took such delight in the lives of Samuel, Anna, Chloé, Théo, Maïa, Rachel and Lilou. and now the arrival of four great grand-children, Louane, Sacha, Elise and Jade. She loved to host or attend parties, to encourage the young to entertain with music and plays.

She was always such good fun. After a wonderful dinner and musical evening in the Alps with the whole family just a few years ago Monica was to be found waking up the surprised manager of her firmly locked hotel at one in the morning—he had made the big mistake thinking the gracious great-grandmother would be tucked up in bed early and didn't need a night key!

Third identity was British. Back in London and with her children grown up, Monica studied English Literature at Birkbeck College, the University of London, being awarded a first class degree. She also put her French to good use working as an interpreter for companies doing business between France and Britain. From the 1980s John and Monica made their home in Wimbledon. It was a wonderful, welcoming, humorous, sociable and sometimes argumentative world—and I felt privileged to be welcomed into it so completely.

Monica was a committed member of the Wimbledon Society, editing the newsletter in 2005 for four years. Her love of books led her to pioneer literary walks for the Society. She worked tirelessly with publishers to get big name authors such as William Hague, Max Hastings and Penelope Lively. She loved finding connections with Wimbledon—linking a new book on Nelson with the many sites associated with his life. She was also a great supporter of the Wimbledon Book Fest.

And Monica's love of history led to the launch in 2013 of the Richard Milward Essay award for local history, in honour of a great local historian and past president of the Wimbledon Society. She loved walking on the Common and in Cannizaro Park. There are now two trees in memory of Monica and John on the Common opposite Cannizaro House.

We can't choose how we die—but Monica fought her cancer with great courage and good humour. Her last days were in her own home and surrounded by family. And we can choose how we live, and Monica was a woman who said yes to life—yes to family and friends, yes to history, music, culture and the arts, yes to France, yes to Ireland, yes to Britain and yes to Wimbledon. She made the very most of all her identities. She lives on in our hearts.

Richard Tait, Sacred Heart Church, Wimbledon, 27 January 2022

17 August 2021

[A round robin.]

Dearest folk at home in Oz or abroad,

tributes to Maev continue to arrive. From Wimbledon Monica Ellison wrote: she was 'one, big, unforgettable personality and I feel fortunate to have met her'. The other day I googled Maev O'Collins, and found a pleasing amount of well-ordered material about her life, achievements, and publications. No errors, gross or otherwise, turned up. Check that out and you will see what I mean.

I engaged in this googling as I have been asked to write around 600 words for a column, 'And finally...', which closes every issue of *The Expository Times*. I thought: why not write on Maev, and kick off with a poignant statement of the Irish writer John McGahern about the early death of his beloved mother Susan? 'She doesn't answer to her name anymore.'

The *ExTim*, founded in the 1890s and based in Edinburgh, has been very friendly to me, accepting so far for publication half a dozen articles. And now they want me to write a column, which resembles the 'Thought for the Day' for the BBC. 'Maev is a good topic', I thought.

The extended lockdown means that I continue locked out of sharing in burgers along the Yarra Boulevard on Sunday evenings [I refer to the hamburgers that Jim Peters, a nephew, prepared every Sunday evening]. Come on, COVID-19, give me a break. You have won the world title. Why not loosen up on life in Parkville and Kew? Surely relations should be encouraged between those two locales.

This morning I headed for a cardiologist, Ron Dick of Epworth Hospital. He looked after my brother Jim towards the end his life. Yes, Jim's medical connections continue to show up. Earlier this year some urological attention came my way from David Clarke, who did training with Jim years ago and, like him, happily seems to believe 'the quicker the better'.

One of my colleagues here in Parkville served in the South Vietnam marines, and was there for the fall of Saigon in 1975. His background makes his remarks about the fall of Kabul even more interesting.

Much love and every blessing, Gerald.

23 August 2021.

Liebster Gerald!

Sorry I couldn't make the family zoom yesterday [with Jim, Sally, and their family]. I was out on a Covid-safe bushwalk and did not have any service on my phone. Hopefully I can be there for the next one.

Lockdown is very bearable, now that the uni is back. I am on the editing team for the Wesley College Yearbook and a UniSyd student journal called '1978'. It's keeping me busy at my desk all day. In the afternoons I go running laps around St John's oval, even though it is technically closed. The other day I was doing laps and I got kicked off! Crazy considering all we are allowed to do is walk and run around at the moment, and campus security is pre-occupied with the wellbeing of the grass.

I hope all is well in Parkville. You've got lots to look forward to. September/October has always been my favourite time in Melbourne. I can imagine all the flowers out the back [of Jesuit Theological College] basking in the sun; the sound of traffic on the way to the airport; the quiet clink of plates in the kitchen. Hopefully you are not too bored in lockdown [our sixth]. Have you gotten your vaccine?

I am writing another article for *Australian Catholics*, similar to the last few creative ones. It's a love story between Mary and Joseph.

I am approaching it cautiously, because the story doesn't exactly fit our modern conception of 'love'—a huge age gap, the concept of the value of virginity, surprise impregnation, and the arranged marriage part are pretty red hot topics around here. But obviously it's so much more complex, and I don't want to hide from these things or change the story. I'm thinking of pinpointing some moments in their story when they discover things about each other and build trust. I've been doing some reading up on Joseph's past (especially the adventures in Egypt—wow!) to get an idea of what kind of a guy he was. Any suggestions about parts of the Bible that could add to my research on this topic?

Can't wait to get back to Melbourne to see you again. Lots of love, Nevie.

29 August 2021.

[A letter to my nephew Steve in Malaysia and niece Joanna in the USA.]

Dearest Joanna and Steve, On Sunday last in a Zoom meeting, after many years I heard again that quote from Garrison Keillor: 'Welcome to Lake Wobegon where all the women are strong, all the men good-looking, and all the children above average.' Has GK's humour lasted?

Recently a Jesuit friend, told me how serious and nervous he felt when meeting Pope Francis for the first time. The Pope took his hand, looked straight into his eyes, and said: 'Smile. Smile please.' The two of them burst out laughing.

It's nearly two months since Maev left us. The tributes to her have often highlighted her heroic and innovative work in Papua

New Guinea. One thing I refrained from mentioning was her being conceived in PNG. In late 1928 Father was up there on legal business for the administrator Sir Hubert Murray (brother of the Oxford classical scholar Gilbert Murray), and he took Mother with him for a break from looking after their first two little children. Once or twice I suggested to Maev that her love for PNG, which flowered when she took a university appointment there in 1972, was a case of déjà vu. She did not deny my claim but never enthused over the mysterious connection I was suggesting.

Last Tuesday I followed the funeral Mass (in a Neutral Bay (Sydney) church) of my cousin Patrick Lewis (born 24 October 1930). His mother, Mary Glynn, was Mother's sister. A Sydney priest, Tony Doherty, three or four years younger than Patrick, who first got to know him when they were fellow boarders at St Ignatius College, Riverview in the early 1940s, celebrated the Mass with a loving simplicity that brought back all kinds of memories. The first volume of my autobiography has much to recall about Patrick's mother Mary, Patrick himself, and Barbara Coleman whom he married around 1972 and who died (of cancer) around 2008. It was a heart attack that carried Patrick away. He had been deeply and affectionately concerned about how I was coping with Maev's death. He followed on streaming her funeral Mass, and ensured that his adopted daughter (Susanti) and her husband came in from the hills outside Melbourne to attend the funeral. And now he has suddenly departed and—what I feel very much—there is no one to talk with about the going of this dear friend and cousin. Moira and Maev are dead, and I can't talk with Susanti, as she is presumably quarantined somewhere. At least she was allowed to cross the border to New South Wales and, as the only eulogist, spoke so movingly of Patrick; like him she is a social worker.

Too bad we cannot get together. But here at least are some musings and news.

With very much love, Gerald.

[To Kenneth Woodward, for several decades religion editor of Newsweek.]

22 September 2021.

Dear Ken,

I am just back from a brief stint (three days) in Epworth Hospital, which gave me the chance to finish reading your *Getting God*, a compelling account of American faith, culture and politics from the age of Eisenhower to the ascent of Trump. All those vivid passages in your book brought back experiences of the US after I first arrived in the fall of 1968. It also filled in large gaps; there was much I failed to take on board from 1968 down to my last visit to the States in 2010. I am most grateful for your exceptional book.

You also lit up for me a chapter in the life of my beloved sister Maev, who died earlier this year. In 1967 she settled in New York to study for a doctorate in social work at Columbia University. She experienced at first hand the assassination of Martin Luther King and Robert Kennedy. In those years her letters filled in the picture of what, as an international student, she tried to do for the civil rights movement—in particular, the Poor People's Campaign. She never raised questions about the 'unredeemed' title of my 1969 book, *Man and His New Hopes*, but seemed to approve thoroughly of its contents.

At Episcopal Theological College [Boston], Harvey Cox launched the book with 140 in attendance and a TV crew visiting from Germany and filming the discussion for home consumption. During the five years of teaching for the Weston School of Theology (in the Boston Theological Institute) I saw a good deal of Harvey, and later he visited me in Rome. I was glad to dedicate some pages to him in *A Midlife Journey* (Connor Court Publishing, 2012).

Your book contains so much that I would love to take up, such as what you wrote about the interest in death and dying (1968-72). You reminded me of the work of Ned Cassem, SJ, (1935-2015), who spent his life at Massachusetts General Hospital and was widely acknowledged for his work/ministry for dying patients. Ned enlisted me in a team-taught course on death during my years at Weston (1968-72).

Your book is a gem; many thanks for it. Incidentally, your editor at Doubleday, Gary Jansen, proved himself top-class for *Seek God Everywhere*, an edition that I prepared with two American Jesuits of Anthony de Mello's lectures on St Ignatius's Spiritual Exercises.

Every blessing, Ken, to you, Betty and your whole family, Gerry.

[To my niece in San Francisco, Dr Marion Peters.]

8 November 2021

Dearest Marion,

At the Jesuit Theological College we inaugurated Sunday brunch at ten o'clock. It has proved a dramatic success, albeit the coffee is still too strong. I will take charge of that next Sunday. Yes, eggs, bacon, beans, cocktail tomatoes, onions, toast and the rest matched the choices of the classical Australian brunch.

On the second Sunday, the brunch provided a break for a small boy (Bill) and his mother, who had come up from Tasmania for his heart operation and were naturally a bit nervous about the procedure which he faced. But our resident priest-doctor (Hoa) assured me that this is a 'normal' operation which closes holes and in other ways assures regular heart growth. Bill's mother, the wife of an agricultural scientist, seems to know only one person in Melbourne, Jamie Calder, a Jesuit psychologist who belongs to our community and works for Australian Catholic University. The hospital is only a loud shout across Royal Park from the Jesuit Theological College. Good luck, Bill. The op seems to have gone well.

On last Friday night we watched the first part of *Gone with the Wind* (1939), which I had never seen before, despite its running for many weeks in one of Dad's cinemas. Perhaps at eight I was thought too young to be exposed to Clark Gable and Vivien Leigh. Last night we watched the second part. Despite the lapse of years and racist overtones, it has not lost the Wow factor.

In 2009, just before I flew back to Melbourne from Wimbledon, I did the funeral for Mary Stewart. She had done her schooling at the Convent of the Sacred Heart, Roehampton, and liked to recall her days there with Vivien Leigh, a boarder from India: 'she was just wild.' Two years older than Leigh, a friend at the same school and much more 'proper' was Maureen O'Sullivan. Known for playing Jane to Tarzan in various films, O'Sullivan had numerous children, including Mia Farrow, who lived it out with Woody Allen. As you can imagine, Mary's stories found a rapt hearer in me.

Becoming bored by writing articles, I have started a book on the

Spiritual Exercises of St Ignatius Loyola. I twice taught a course on that material, and may have something useful to say. Ignatius's work is a classic, but there have been only two or three significant books on it during the last twenty years: one is by a deceased Indian (Anthony de Mello) whose lectures on the Exercises were edited posthumously by Dan Kendall, Jeffrey LaBelle, and myself, and the other is a radically revised, longish work of superb value published by an old Spaniard scholar who taught in Madrid. Classics should not drop off the screen of our attention. Justin Peters (a surgeon nephew) and the Epworth Hospital team will have to keep me alive until I finish the ms. on Ignatius.

Blessings to all your dear family.

Peace, with much love and good cheer in the Lord, Gerald.

December 2021.

[For the final issue of *The Expository Times* in 2021.]

'And Finally...Left Alone'

'She didn't answer to her name anymore.' John McGahern was writing of the death of his beloved mother Susan. These words constantly came to mind when my only surviving sibling died last July. 'Maev doesn't answer to her name anymore.'

My parents had six children—three girls and then three boys. Maev was the third daughter and remained single. 'If you don't plan to marry, have an interesting life', Mother told her.

After studies at the Universities of Melbourne and Sydney, she became an outstanding social worker in Melbourne and champion of vulnerable people. In 1967 a scholarship took her to the United States where she completed a PhD at Columbia University and taught at Hunter College.

During Maev's years in New York I was lecturing for Weston School of Theology within the Boston Theological Institute. Yes, she did come north to visit me. But she preferred me down in New York and supporting various causes. One weekend she welcomed a group of Australian aborigines visiting the United Nations. During the campaign against joining the war in Vietnam, the FBI raided her church and arrested Philip Berrigan, the brother of Dan Berrigan. She would pop over to Harlem and take African American boys and girls out for some project or celebration.

One evening Maev entertained a delegation from Papua New Guinea. It included Michael Somare, soon to be PNG's chief minister and later Sir Michael. Over dinner, he invited her to teach at PNG's new university, adding with a smile: 'If you get sick of us or we get sick of you, it's not far to go home.'

Maev took up a post in the Department of Anthropology and Sociology at the University of PNG. In 1972 that university was growing fast to educate a new nation. Maev steered the social work courses towards fostering development, embracing concepts of justice, and eradicating colonial-era structures that had survived independence. She introduced large components of field work, forged cross-cultural alliances among students by assigning them far from their home province, and spent months each year in remote villages working with them.

In 1987, Maev was awarded an MBE by the PNG government 'for

services to the community and education'. She took pride in a letter from Sir Julius Chan, another PNG Prime Minister, who said he was 'fully aware of the work, thought and affection you have given Papua New Guinea and her people over the years'.

When Maev reached the mandatory retirement age, she moved to Canberra and took up an appointment as a fellow at the Australian National University. She began consulting for the United Nations. Her most enjoyable role was police training, which took her around the Pacific and opened up many opportunities to promote development. Later she joined Australian Catholic University and played a significant role in founding its School of Social Work, with branches in Sydney and Brisbane, as well as in Canberra.

She was a wonderful presence in the lives of countless friends and relatives, not least her nineteen nephews and nieces. 'For us', one of them said, 'Maev transformed the mundane into the magical and the everyday into a great adventure'.

The only survivor of six siblings, I have been left the 'one man standing'. Maev doesn't answer to her name anymore. But I draw great comfort from St Augustine:

'All shall be Amen and Alleluia. We shall rest and we shall see.

We shall see and we shall know. We shall know and we shall love.

We shall love and we shall praise. Behold our end which is no end.'

24 November 2021

[To the German theologian Jürgen Moltmann, Tübingen.]

Lieber Jürgen,

A Happy Thanksgiving to those in the USA and their loving fans elsewhere. Then a blessed Advent, Christmas and New Year to all and sundry.

Last Sunday I shared an early Christmas lunch with the students of Newman College, University of Melbourne. At my table I met an Afghan ('Ali'), who spent many years in exile in Pakistan and is now entering his final year of medical studies at the University of Melbourne, and an indigenous Australian girl who intends to take a month of her Christmas holidays working for aboriginal people who suffer social problems in and around Melbourne. The two students symbolized for me something of the suffering and hardship that Jesus came to share. But I could not say this to them.

At the level of what we eat, an Italian workman, a plasterer and painter, who turns up every two or three years to fix some wall or ceiling in one of the ten terrace houses that make up Jesuit Theological College, started Christmas early for my community. In October he gave us some panettone, which we consumed at once. A violation of Italian food customs? But in a good cause.

At the end of 2021, it seems above all the year that took people away from me: my sister Maev, who died in July, and my oldest friend, James ('Jim') Gobbo, who started boarding school with me at Xavier College in 1944 and died earlier this month. They don't answer to their names any more. With Maev's death, I am the last of my six siblings still standing. Jim received a Rhodes scholarship, became a Supreme Court judge, and finished as Governor of the State of Victoria. Over the years we met in Rome, and I reconnected with him when I returned to Melbourne in 2009.

With two shots for the anti-Covid-19 vaccination, I will remember 2021 as the year of the two deaths and the two jabs.

Next Sunday I preach at the first Mass of an Anglican friend, Russell Goulbourne, an alumnus of Keble, a former faculty member of Kings College, London, and now the dean of the faculty of arts at the University of Melbourne. Russell was a great friend of the late Bishop Geoffrey Rowell, and that gave me a flying start in getting to know Russell.

With loving best wishes for Christmas and the New Year, Gerry.

6

Lockdown Living

The pandemic arrived in March 2020. A month later I wrote from Melbourne to Josef and Ingrid Nolte, German friends (21 April 2020): 'we are stuck with this virus for a long haul'. Looking back after nearly two years and just liberated from the sixth lockdown, what should I say at the end of 2021?

I still wonder about the motives for the panic-buying of toilet rolls at the outbreak of the pandemic in early 2020. What specific anxiety drove people to that particular, irrational response? I must put that question to a Jesuit psychologist (with two doctorates!) who has recently joined our community and teaches on campuses up and down the country.

Spiritual Advice

For eighteen months and more, spiritual writers have gifted me with their messages to survive and even profit by COVID-19: 'stop a minute, quieten down, focus on the presence of God around and within, talk with the Lord'.

Then 'find the words to speak about Christ and his Church'.

'Cultivate a dynamic relationship with the Lord and then you will be able to help people who are spiritually bankrupt and infuriated.' 'We must care for one another and for the stranger; so many people are hit by deep anxiety, shock, and fear.' 'We are facing a new scenario for co-existence.'

In a new Sunday situation, like the one recently imposed, when I could not attend a beautifully sung Eucharist at 11 a.m. either at St Francis Church, Melbourne, or at Newman College, University of Melbourne, I read: 'churches are not being closed. Buildings are being closed. You are the Church. You are to remain open.'

Television images powerfully reinforced a sense of the strange loneliness along with a new unity that was prevailing around the world. Having lived and taught in Rome from 1973 until 2006, I was used to about 25,000 visitors flooding each day into the eternal city. A documentary of Rome brought only the sound of ambulance sirens. Up north in Milan the blind tenor Andrea Bocelli stood alone in the Cathedral when on 13 April 2020 he sang *Panis Angelicus* and *Ave Maria*. So far this streamed 'music for hope' has been heard by over 42 million people.

Sacred Music

Bocelli initiated me into listening to sacred music excellently performed and reaching me on my computer from some wonderfully beautiful setting. When time came for praying, I often begin now with the Taizé hymn *Laudate Dominum* being sung to assemble the people for the Eucharist in the Cathedral of Notre Dame in Paris on 2 August 2019. Or else I listen to 'All People that on Earth Do Dwell' from Hull Munster with a trumpet fanfare, sung on D Day 2013.

'Dear Lord and Father of Mankind', for many Christians the most beautiful hymn available, has come to me from a crowded Westminster Abbey. The royals were also there also in St Paul's Cathedral on 26 January 2021 for a service recalling the 72 persons who perished in Grenfell Tower, a block of flats in West London where the flammable exterior cladding exacerbated a fire which had broken out through an electrical fault. A massive tragedy lent special force to 'Be Still, my Soul (Finlandia)'.

It was not until the outbreak of the pandemic that I realized how much spiritually powerful music, performed by choirs, soloists, and orchestras in some of the most majestic and beautiful buildings in the world is always accessible to me. My first pandemic Christmas was mitigated by the discovery that the classic carols, sung by the choir of King's College, Cambridge, were all waiting for me on my desktop.

In these and many other ways the pandemic, along with great suffering and numerous deaths, has also brought blessings. It enhanced my admiration for two Vietnamese Jesuits, blood brothers with whom I live and who run a centre for Vietnamese Catholics in Melbourne. Using the extra time forced upon me, I interviewed them and produced an article submitted to the *The Pastoral Review* for 2022. Let me finish this book with a small tribute to two courageous and saintly brothers.

The Brothers Pham

For years I have been blessed by sharing the same community with two Vietnamese brothers, both Jesuits and ordained priests: Minh-Uoc Pham (b. 1952) and Van Ai Pham (b. 1956). Separately they faced extreme danger when crossing the Gulf of Thailand, an inlet of the South China Sea, to find a new home. They became valued Australian citizens, without ceasing to be devout Catholics and genuine Vietnamese.

In a world where priests from other continents frequently staff parishes and other pastoral centres, it is worth telling the story of the brothers Pham. It should encourage parishioners to hear and be inspired by the experiences of foreign-born clergy.

Living in the north of Vietnam during the Second World War, the Pham family knew deep suffering when the Japanese invaded in 1943. A severe famine killed the grandfather of the brothers.

When the country was divided in 1954, their family, along with many other Catholics, fled to the South. They settled in the Mekong delta.

Minh-Uoc, an outstanding high school student, constantly topped his class. He had completed two years of university study in Saigon, when he began training at the military academy and then transferred as a young lieutenant to the elite South Vietnam Marines. In March 1972 they began fierce fighting with the enemy forces to retake the Quang Tri Citadel. On 15 September, 1,500 North Vietnamese surrendered.

He smiles at the Communist fake news: 'there were only 21,000 of us; they claimed to have killed 26,000 marines, more than actually existed. Some must have died twice.'

It was a bitter blow when the war ended in 1975. 'Saigon surrendered on 30 April. It didn't fall', Minh-Uoc always insists. He took off his uniform, and endured three years of 're-education' in a labour camp.

Lockdown Living

'We played soccer against the guards', he recalls. 'We always had to let them win'.

Shortly after his release from the camp, Vietnam attacked Cambodia, and Minh-Uoc was drafted into the invading forces as an unarmed worker. 'You survived the first time', his mother said. 'You won't survive a second time'.

With others, Minh-Uoc gathered gold and other valuables from friends. It took them two months to buy the materials and build the boat. They used the engine of an old military truck and bought diesel fuel, hidden at once for their departure.

When departure-day came in 1980, almost all of the 47 escapees, half of them women and children, had reached the boat when they were discovered by the Communist police and had to leave at once. Minh-Uoc was still on his way through the night with a teenage boy. After two hours of desperate rowing, in 'the dark jungle of the Mekong Delta', he managed to link up with his party.

Out on the Gulf of Thailand, their ten-day run to Malaysia was interrupted by Thai pirates armed with rifles. Minh-Uoc threw his revolver into the sea but forgot the ammunition inside his vest. Discovering the bullets, two pirates were about to bayonet him. 'Lord, take my soul', he prayed. 'I entrust myself to you.' At the last moment the group leader stopped his men.

After the pirates left, the Vietnamese approached the Malaysian shore—weak, thirsty, and hungry. Arriving close to a military base, they faced strong opposition before being allowed to land and spend the night on the beach.

The following morning the Red Crescent came and ferried them to a refugee camp. American, Australian, and Canadian officials offered placements in their countries. A Jesuit novice in Minh-

Uoc's group suggested that he write to the superior general of the Jesuits, Fr. Pedro Arrupe, who had founded the Jesuit Refugee Service. At once Arrupe contacted the Jesuit provincial in Australia and a Vietnamese Jesuit who had reached Adelaide a few years earlier. They both offered help. After a month in a Kuala Lumpur transit camp, Minh-Uoc arrived in Adelaide (South Australia) on 21 September 1980.

The following March he entered the Society of Jesus and was ordained in 1990. His ministry has taken him to parishes and schools. He has worked as assistant to the Tertian director, who leads an international group of Jesuits in their last, spiritual year before final vows.

A year after his brother reached Australia, on 28 February 1982 Ai Pham made his run for it. On a river boat, just nine metres long and 1.7 metres wide and powered by a small engine, he joined 37 family friends. He had a special responsibility for a cousin, who brought a three-year old child and an eight-month-old child. Her husband escaped three months later with Ai's younger sister.

Once the party moved into international waters on the evening of 2 March, they hit very rough seas. The following day a Thai fishing boat attacked at ten in the morning.

The fishermen stole anything they could find. They beat the Vietnamese escapees, and knocked Ai unconscious. When he returned to consciousness, he glimpsed the utter terror on the face of his cousin—a picture that has stayed with him for a lifetime.

The fishermen demanded dollars, good American dollars. All that Ai could pull from his pockets were notes carrying the picture of Ho Chi Minh.

The Vietnamese became more terrified when they spotted two

other Thai fishing boats approaching around 4 pm. Half an hour later salvation arrived.

A humanitarian German ship, the 'Cap Anamur', appeared on the horizon, changed course, and headed straight for the scene of piracy. Expertly it took on board the Vietnamese and then destroyed their river boat. The Thai fishermen watched their prey disappear into the safety of a converted cargo ship. Ai always carries in his wallet a photo of the 'Cap Anamur'.

The director of the German operation, a medical doctor and former Jesuit, Dr Rupert Neudeck (1939–2016), had organized the mission. He employed a German captain, an engineer, a navigator, other officers, a doctor, two nurses, and a crew of Filipino sailors.

Since 'Cap Anamur' had just swept into the Gulf of Thailand at the start of that particular mission, Ai, his cousin, her two children, and the other Vietnamese remained on board for two months and two days. The ship rescued refugees from ten other boats. All in all, it saved 230 people before heading for the Philippines. On 5 May 1982, it deposited its precious cargo at the Palawan Refugee Camp, built on an island about one hour by air south-west of Manila. Eventually, the German mission rescued 11, 000 refugees.

Ai, his cousin, and her children were welcomed to Australia. The others went to Berlin and Frankfurt. Two years later, on the 6 March 1984, he followed his call to become a Jesuit and entered the novitiate. He was ordained a priest on 27 November 1993.

Ai's studies culminated in a doctorate in theology at Boston College. Now an Australian citizen, he returned to Vietnam in 2004 to Saint Joseph's Jesuit Scholasticate, Saigon. He worked there as lecturer (2004–2015) and also as Dean of Theology (2009–2015). He helped revive the theological program disrupted by war and political changes. He shaped the program according to Jesuit formation requirements and affiliated it academically with the Loyola School of Theology (LST) in Manila. Ai also found time to work as a Jesuit formator and lecturer at LST (2006–09), called there by Fr Adolfo Nicholás, who led the Jesuits of Eastern Asia and Oceania. Before becoming superior general of the Jesuit Order in 2008. 'Nico' also invited Minh-Uoc to become his personal assistant for several years in Manila and rector of a house of formation.

Like Minh-Uoc, Ai copes very well with the pastoral ministry and now serves as assistant to his brother as chaplain for the large Vietnamese Catholic Community based in Flemington. It is close to the legendary race course which hosts each November the Melbourne Cup, 'the race that stops the nation'.

For major feast days, both brothers celebrate Mass and preach for Melbourne YouTube programs that reach Vietnamese around Australia, in North America, and elsewhere (including Vietnam itself with its population of nearly one hundred million). Their programs 'score' fifty thousand hits and more. Recently Ai heard from an uncle living in North Vietnam who followed his Mass on YouTube.

Minh-Uoc and Ai have lived a life of heroic pilgrims. A deep Catholic faith has been the key, along with an unbreakable love for their family. A peace and joy in their priestly vocation come through when they smile and laugh so easily.

Some Relatives and Friends Mentioned in the Letters

The children of Kevin and Dympna (my sister) Coleman (both deceased): Les, Nicholas, Dympna Mary, and Dominic (deceased).

The children of Dominic Coleman and Josie Millard: Edmund ('Ned') and Antigone ('Annie').

Monica Ellison, a cousin who lived in Wimbledon, UK.

Maev O'Collins, my youngest sister, two years older than me.

The children of James and Moira (my sister) Peters with their spouses: Stewart and Nola Peters. Marion Peters and Eric ('Rick') Brown, Justin and Jill Peters (and their daughters Elizabeth ('Lizzie') and Anna), Joanna Peters, Bronwen Peters, James ('Jim') and Sally Peters, Stephen Peters and Marianne Lim, and their daughter Samantha ('Sam')

The children of Jim and Sally Peters: Marion, William ('Billy'), and Genevieve ('Nevie').

Mary Venturini, a journalist friend who, in retirement, has left Rome to live on the island of Jersey.

Laura Zampetti, an Italian friend who now lives in Montenegro and works for the European Union.

INDEX OF NAMES

Alberigo, Giuseppe, historian 83
Allen, Woody, film director 106
Andrews, Daniel, premier 22, 49
Anselm of Canterbury, saint 39
Aristotle, philosopher 31
Arrupe, Pedro, superior general of Jesuits 128
Augustine of Hippo, Saint 92, 109

Bach, Johann Sebastian, composer 69, 70
Barker, Sue, tennis commentator 31
Barnes, Julian, writer 51, 58, 59
Bartlett, Michael, friend 92
Berrigan, Daniel, Jesuit 91, 108
Berrigan, Philip, brother of Daniel 91, 108
Boccaccio. Giovanni, writer 58
Bocelli, Andrea, tenor 114
Bonfigli, Benedetto, painter 65–66
Botticelli, Sandro, painter 66–67
Bowden, John, publisher 79 n.
Boyd, Martin, novelist 55
Branagh, Kenneth, actor, 43
Brennan, Frank, Jesuit, 42n
Bridges, Robert, poet, 70
Broadbent, Jim, actor 51
Brown, Eric (Rick), husband of Marion Peters 121
Brownell, Sonia, wife of George Orwell 23

Bruegel the Elder, Pieter, painter 67
Byrne, Brendan, Jesuit 73

Calder, Jamie, Jesuit 74, 106
Calduch Benages, Nuria, scriptural scholar 10, 12, 89
Campbell, William (Willie), ophthalmologist 43
Camus, Albert, novelist 39
Capp, Sally, mayor 19
Cash, Pat, tennis player 31
Cassem, Ned, Jesuit 105
Catullus, poet 50
Chadwick, Henry, historian 83
Chan, Sir Julius, prime minister 109
Chenu, Marie-Dominique, theologian 17
Clark, Manning, historian 93
Clarke, David, surgeon 86, 100
Clement XIV, pope 87
Coakley, Sarah, theologian 73
Cobb, Richard, historian 95
Coleman, Antigone (Annie), grand-niece 24, 85, 121
Coleman, Barbara, friend 103
Coleman, Dominic, nephew 24, 33, 92, 121
Coleman, Dympna Mary *see* Painter, Dympna Mary
Coleman, Edmund (Ned), grand-nephew 31, 121

Coleman, Les, nephew 24, 121
Coleman, Nicholas (Nick), nephew 24, 36, 121
Collins, Lady Priscilla, publisher 83
Collins, Sir William, publisher 83
Congar, Yves, theologian 76, 83
Courier, Jim, tennis player 31
Cox, Harvey, theologian 105
Crilly, Donna, publisher 46
Curtin, Stephen (Steve), Jesuit 9, 38, 74

Dante Alighieri, genius 12–13, 49
Davis, Jack, aboriginal leader 91
Davis, Stephen, philosopher 46
De Beauvoir, Simone, philosopher 22
De Mauny, Erik, journalist 94
De Mello, Anthony, Jesuit 46, 105, 107
Dick, Ron, cardiologist, 100
Dinh, Hoa, Jesuit 73, 106
Dockery, Michelle, actress 51
Doherty, Tony, priest 103
Donati, Piccarda, featured by Dante 13
Donne, John, poet 68, 69
Doria Podgson Pamphilj, Princess Gesine 39–40
Doria Pamphilj, Massimiliano, husband of Gesine 39–40
Dreyfus, Alfred, victim 58
Dupuis, Jacques, Jesuit 46, 81

Eisenhower, President Dwight 104
Eliot, George, novelist 51
Eliot, T. S., poet 22, 69
Elliott, Amanda, racing patron 28
Ellison, Charlotte, cousin 97
Ellison, Emma, cousin 97
Ellison, Jane, cousin 97
Ellison, John, husband of Monica 96–99
Ellison, Juliet, cousin 97
Ellison, Monica, beloved cousin 10, 13, 85–86, 94–99, 121

Faggioli, Massimo, theologian 15
Feuerbach, Ludwig, philosopher 81
Francis, Pope, God's gift 11, 15, 40, 46, 59, 102
Fraser, Malcolm, prime minister 56, 93
Freud, Sigmund, psychologist 81

Gable, Clark, actor 106
Geertgen Tot Sint Jans, painter 67
Gerhardt, Paul, composer 69
Gly
Glynn, Mary, aunt 103
Glynn, Justin, Jesuit 74
Glynn, Patrick (Paddy) McMahon, grandfather 19, 30
Gobbo, Sir James (Jim), oldest friend 110–11
Goulbourne, Russell, priest 111
Graf, Bernhard, anaesthetist 10, 71–72
Graf, Josef, auxiliary bishop 71

Index

Graf, Steffi, surgeon 10, 71–72
Greer, Germaine, feminist 60
Grünewald, Mathias, painter 66

Hague, William, writer 99
Harbison, Janet, cousin 95
Hastings, Max, historian 99
Henderson, Anne, historian 19, 30
Henderson, Gerard, journalist 19
Hendrick, Richard, Franciscan 38–39
Homer, epic poet 55
Horace, poet 50

Ignatius Loyola, saint 58, 107

James, Clive, poet 16
Jansen, Gary 105
John XXIII, saint 76
John Paul II, saint 46
Joyce, James, novelist 29

Kaiser, Robert, journalist 76
Kamel, Georg Joseph, Jesuit 57
Kasper, Walter, cardinal 80
Keillor, Garrison, writer 102
Kemp, David, historian 93
Kendall, Anne, sister of Daniel 47
Kendall, Daniel, Jesuit 10–11, 30, 35–36, 45–48, 60, 107
Kennedy, Robert, presidential candidate 104
Kentenich, Josef 51

King, Martin Luther 104
King, Nicholas, Jesuit 73
Knox, James, cardinal 78, 79
König, Frans, cardinal 80
Krushchev, Nikita, premier of the USSR 59
Küng, Hans, theologian 10, 12, 76–83

LaBelle, Jeffrey, Jesuit 46, 107
Lafitte, Jean, archbishop 29
Larkin, Philip, poet 51, 59
Lasch, Christopher, sociologist 26
Lee, Dorothy, biblical scholar 73
Leigh, Vivien, actress 106
Lewis, Patrick, cousin 103
Lewis, Susanti, daughter of Patrick 103
Lim, Marianne, wife of Steve Peters 10, 16
Lively, Penelope, writer 99
Lonergan, Bernard, Jesuit 24, 77
Lyons, Enid, wife of Joseph 19
Lyons, Joseph, prime minister 19

Martini, Carlo Maria, cardinal 45
Marx, Karl, philosopher 81
McArdle, Patrick, academic leader 90
McEnroe, John, tennis player 31
McGahern, John, writer 100, 107
McGahern, Susan, mother of John 100, 107
McGarty, Bernard, priest 47-48

McVeigh, Michael, journalist 21
Metz, Johann Baptist, theologian 82
Milne, A. A., writer 49
Milton, John, poet 68, 69
Moltmann, Jürgen, theologian 10, 54-55
Murray, Gilbert, classical scholar 103
Murray, Sir Hubert, colonial administrator 103
Murray, Robert, Jesuit 93

Nelson, Horatio, admiral 99
Neudeck, Rupert, medical doctor 119
Newman, John Henry, saint 29
Nguyen, Cao, Jesuit 74
Nicholas, Adolfo, superior general of Jesuits 120
Nighy, Bill, actor 35
Nolte, Ingrid, wife of Josef 10, 41-42, 113
Nolte, Josef, theologian 10, 41-42, 113

O'Collins, Ellie, niece 92-93
O'Collins, Frank, nephew 38-39
O'Collins, James (Jim) Patrick, brother 43, 86, 100
O'Collins, Joan, mother 103
O'Collins, Maev, sister 10-13, 15, 24-25, 29, 36, 40, 87, 90-92, 94, 100, 102-03, 107-10
O'Collins, Patrick Francis (Frank), father 103, 106
O'Collins, Victoria (Tori), niece 10, 74-75, 92-93
O'Connell, Daniel, liberator 96
O'Hanlon, Daniel, Jesuit 76
Olivier, Laurence, actor 43
O'Neill, Brett, Jesuit 10, 72-74
Orwell, George, writer 21, 23
O'Sullivan, Maureen, actress 106

Paine, Tim, cricketer 23
Painter, Dympna Mary, niece 13, 55-56
Parnell, Charles, Irish leader 96
Paul VI, saint 77, 78, 83
Payne, Michelle, jockey 25, 30
Pell, George, cardinal 41, 42n, 58
Peters, Anna, grand-niece 16, 121
Peters, Bronwen, niece 55-56, 121
Peters, Elizabeth (Lizzie), grand-niece 74, 121
Peters, Genevieve (Nevie), *passim*
Peters, James W. S. (Jim), nephew 15-17, 23, 28, 35, 37, 49, 59, 61, 86-87, 100-01, 121
Peters, Jill, wife of Justin 16, 74, 121
Peters, Joanna 10, 102, 121
Peters, Justin, nephew 16, 74, 107, 121
Peters, Marion, niece 10, 60, 105-07, 121
Peters, Moira, sister 78, 121
Peters, Nola, wife of Stewart Peters 18, 121
Peters, Sally, wife of James Peters

Index

15–17, 35, 101, 121
Peters, Samantha (Sam), grand-niece 16, 121
Peters, Stephen (Steve), nephew 10, 16, 41, 102, 121
Peters, Stewart, nephew 18, 121
Peters, William (Billy), grand-nephew 10–11, 16, 31, 37, 41
Pham, Ai, Jesuit 60, 73, 115–20
Pham, Min-Uoc, Jesuit 74, 115–20
Plato, philosopher 31
Plehwe, Walter, doctor 75
Potter, Lady Primrose, friend 49–50
Power, Pat, bishop 90
Pozzi, Samuel, surgeon 58
Proust, Marcel, writer 52
Pushkin, Alexander, writer 58

Rahner, Karl, Jesuit 83
Rampling, Charlotte, actress 51
Ramsey, Michael, archbishop 78
Rita of Cascia, saint 87
Rowan, Paul, teacher 42
Rowell, Geoffrey, bishop 111

Sargent, John Singer, painter 58
Shakespeare, William, genius 18, 27
Shostakovich, Dmitri, composer 59
Socrates, philosopher 31
Somare, Sir Michael, prime minister 108
Southwell, Robert, saint 68, 69
Stalin, Joseph, dictator 59
Stewart, Mary, friend 106

Stokes, Ben, cricketer 23
Strickland, Liz, wife of Eric de Mauny 94

Tait, Richard, professor of journalism 95–99
Taylor, D. J., writer 23
Teresa of Calcutta, Mother, saint 78–80
Teuffenbach, Alexandra von, theologian 50–51
Thérèse of Lisieux, saint 40
Thompson, Emma, actress 60
Tobin, Michael, undertaker 54
Tromp, Sebastiaan, Jesuit 50–51
Trump, Donald, president 104

Venturini, Mary, journalist 42–43, 121
Virgil, poet 50, 55, 59

Walsh, Brendan, journalist 50
White, Denis, friend 93
Wilde, Oscar, writer 24
Williams, Rowan, archbishop 30
Witherup, Ronald, biblical scholar 73
Woodward, Kenneth, journalist 104-105
Wright, N. T., bishop 74, 85

Zampetti, Laura, friend 10, 13, 86–87, 121
Zhao, Andrew, Jesuit 73, 85

Lettters from the Pandemic

www.ingramcontent.com/pod-product-compliance
Lightning Source LLC
Chambersburg PA
CBHW070400240426
43671CB00013BA/2574